HANDBOOK TO A GRAMMAR FOR BIBLICAL HEBREW

JENNIFER S. GREEN

G. BROOKE LESTER

JOSEPH F. SCRIVNER

Abingdon Press
Nashville

Handbook to a Grammar for Biblical Hebrew

This book is printed on acid-free paper.

Library of Congress Cataloging-in-Publication Data

Green, Jennifer S., 1972–
Handbook to a grammar for Biblical Hebrew / Jennifer S. Green, G. Brooke Lester, Joseph F. Scrivner.
p. cm.
"An annotated answer key to C. L. Seow's ... A grammar for biblical Hebrew (rev. ed.)."
ISBN 0-687-00834-4 (alk. paper)
1. Hebrew language—Grammar—Problems, exercises, etc. I. Lester, G. Brooke, 1966– II. Scrivner, Joseph F., 1969– III. Seow, C. L. (Choon Leong). Grammar for Biblical Hebrew. IV. Title.
PJ4567 .S424 1995 Suppl. 2
492.4'82421—dc22 2004046214

ISBN 13: 978-0-687-00834-6

08 09 10 11 12 13 14—10 9 8 7 6 5 4 3
MANUFACTURED IN THE UNITED STATES OF AMERICA

CONTENTS

Introduction

This Handbook is designed for a single purpose: to help the student make good use of C. L. Seow's *A Grammar for Biblical Hebrew,* whether in the context of classroom instruction or self-study. Toward that end:

- ✦ Terminology, abbreviations, and the like will correspond to that found in *GBH.*
- ✦ Annotations to answer keys will typically cite relevant sections from *GBH* for review.
- ✦ Additional exercises of a certain type are offered but do not dominate. Even these aim to help the student profit from the many and various exercises already found in *GBH.*

For the sake of consistency and ease of use, each lesson includes the same set of five sections: In This Lesson, Terms to Know, Tips, an annotated Answer Key, and Review the Concepts.

In This Lesson: Here the student may see at a glance the major sections of a given lesson and select forms and concepts to be expected in that lesson. Often representative forms will be presented in Hebrew script alongside their grammatical descriptions (e.g., Infinitive Absolute קָטוֹל). This section allows the student an orientation to the lesson about to be learned and also lends itself to "rapid review" of lessons already covered.

Terms to Know: This section lists, alphabetically, important grammatical terms the student should learn or remember in order to engage a given lesson. Every term is taken from *GBH.* If a term is introduced for the first time in the current lesson, it is not followed by a chapter reference. If it is a term already learned but important for the current lesson, it is followed by a chapter reference (not, in this case, to a section or page number; this is necessary because many terms are developed only in the context of an entire lesson).

Tips: Here are offered a few teaching points, culled from the experience of teachers and students who have used *GBH* in the past. These may be thought of as strategies, a guide to oft-used pointers and occasional traps characteristic of the current lesson. Often the student is here introduced to helpful memory devices, warned about possible misconstruals, or otherwise "helped along" in an understanding of the more important grammatical concepts.

Answer Keys: These heavily annotated keys are perhaps the bread and butter of this handbook. An annotated answer key is an invaluable aid both to teacher and student in an introductory language course. Students have the opportunity to check their answers carefully against the keys before the homework is reviewed in class; where they are unable to make sense of the answers provided, they are at least prepared to present their difficulties articulately upon examination. The teacher is freed to make efficient use of limited classtime: rather than simply checking for right or wrong answers, the teacher may press the students regarding their *understanding* of the answers and their comprehension of the relevant material.

The annotations to the answer keys refer in nearly every case to the relevant section and page numbers in *GBH.* Rather than annotate every single answer, the authors have used their judgment in selecting exercises for annotation. In general, the current lesson is referenced in the first few exercises testing a newly learned concept. Previous lessons are referenced wherever the authors have deemed that such might be helpful, such as if the relevant concept is notoriously elusive or if it has not been encountered for several lessons.

The vast majority of references are to *GBH* and always include section and page numbers, such as "VIII.5.b, note ii, pp. 84–85." Several references to BDB are also included as needed, as are occasional references to GKC, Joüon, or *IBHS.*

Exercises involving biblical passages include annotations of two kinds. First, all the glosses from *GBH* are included; these are almost invariably a translation of a word or phrase not yet accessible to the student. Second, many annotations are added to help students navigate elements that are theoretically within their skills but that may require some practical assistance.

Review the Concepts: GBH already boasts an impressive number and variety of exercises, so many that the teacher is able to assign only so many, and of such type that she feels will best suit the particular needs of a given student body. Nevertheless, this handbook offers, for each lesson, a set of exercises filling a special pedagogical niche. Every grammar, *GBH* included, makes use of some special vocabulary, or jargon, to communicate essential concepts: "attributive adjective," "open syllable," "compensatory lengthening," and so forth. Even the student who takes readily to such necessary jargon may at first find it difficult to control these special terms in the heat of translation, as it were, to bring "the rubber to the road."

This section, then, provides exercises designed specifically to rehearse the grammatical vocabulary essential to a given lesson. In the earlier lessons, the focus is simply on promoting familiarity with essential items (character formation, vocal and silent *šĕwāʾ*, gender and number of the noun, etc.). As soon as possible, though, the focus in this section includes not only the terms themselves but helping the student to control these grammatical tools in the process of translation. For example, the student is encouraged to distinguish in translation between the three uses of the participle (attributive, predicative, substantive: lesson VIII). Similarly, attention is given to translating the several uses of the infinitive absolute (lesson XXII).

A word about the translations offered in this handbook: it is axiomatic that every translation is an interpretation. No text affords but a single translation; indeed, it is a milestone in the student's progress when she realizes in practice that every text is patient of several translations, geared toward various readers in disparate contexts. The translations offered here are at best carefully chosen guides, designed to elucidate particular elements of Hebrew grammar.

Afterword: Where Does One Go from Here?

While *A Grammar for Biblical Hebrew* is no substitute for a true reference grammar (see Excursus D, pp. 129–31), it is nonetheless so rich in detail as to serve well for ready reference in the context of intermediate Hebrew. Even the most diligent introductory student will not yet have plumbed the depths of the many notes, examples, and excurses. The table of contents and subject index contain more than adequate detail for this purpose. Students who wish to use *GBH* in post-introductory studies are offered the following suggestions.

One fruitful approach to intermediate biblical Hebrew is "rapid reading." In this exercise one reads long texts, pausing only to resolve such difficulties as utterly confound one's progress. The student should make use of the charted paradigms in the appendix of *GBH* and any other helps that may facilitate rapid progress. In this manner, intermediate students might cover whole books of the Hebrew Bible, enjoying rapid and continuous review of learned biblical Hebrew vocabulary, morphology, and syntax.

Another, supplementary approach is to essay close and exhaustive study of short passages, attempting thereby a comprehensive understanding of a given pericope. Every aspect of morphology and syntax is to be examined, and any uncertainties resolved by means of careful reference to *GBH,* BDB, and *IBHS.* This model would be appropriate for sermon preparation or other careful study of brief texts.

Most teachers of introductory Hebrew will be glad to offer their own tips and suggestions for continued study. Also, many students enjoy regular lunchtime or evening reading sessions with classmates or colleagues.

Congratulations on your successes with introductory Hebrew, and best wishes for your continuing endeavors in Hebrew Bible!

We are grateful to C. L. Seow for his inspiration and encouragement and to the many students who have used and responded to earlier versions of this handbook. We also thank John Kutsko and Bob Buller for their careful editing.

Jennifer S. Green
G. Brooke Lester
Joseph F. Scrivner

Abbreviations

Abbreviations conform in general to those of *A Grammar for Biblical Hebrew* (pp. xi–xii), with two exceptions: some abbreviations have been added, and abbreviations of biblical books conform instead to those of *The SBL Handbook of Style* (Peabody, Mass.: Hendrickson, 1999).

Some of the following abbreviations, though found in *GBH,* may not appear in this handbook. Because the handbook is to be used closely with *GBH,* such abbreviations are nonetheless included in this list as a help to the student.

*	precedes an antecedent, unattested or incorrect form
<	"derives from"
>	"gives rise to"
abs.	absolute state
act.	active
BDB	F. Brown, S. R. Driver, and C. A. Briggs. *A Hebrew and English Lexicon of the Old Testament.* Oxford: Clarendon, 1907 (see *GBH,* Excursus A).
BHS	*Biblia Hebraica Stuttgartensia.* Edited by K. Elliger and W. Rudolph. Stuttgart: Deutsche Bibelgesellschaft, 1983 (see *GBH,* Excursus F).
C	consonant
cp	common plural
coh.	cohortative
consec.	consecutive
cs	common singular
cs.	construct state
du.	dual
fd	feminine dual
fem.	feminine
fp	feminine plural
fs	feminine singular
GBH	C. L. Seow. *A Grammar for Biblical Hebrew.* 2nd rev. ed. Nashville: Abingdon, 1995.

GKC	*Gesenius' Hebrew Grammar*. Edited by E. Kautzsch. Translated by A. E. Cowley. 2nd ed. Oxford: Clarendon, 1910 (see *GBH*, Excursus D).
Hi.	Hiphil
Hisht.	Hishtaphel
Ho.	Hophal
IBHS	B. K. Waltke and M. O'Connor. *An Introduction to Biblical Hebrew Syntax*. Winona Lake, Ind.: Eisenbrauns, 1990.
impf.	imperfect
impv.	imperative
inf.	infinitive
irreg.	irregular
Joüon	P. Joüon. *A Grammar of Biblical Hebrew*. Translated and revised by T. Muraoka. 2 vols. Subsidia biblica 14/1–2. Rome: Pontifical Biblical Institute, 1991.
juss.	jussive
md	masculine dual
mp	masculine plural
ms	masculine singular
MT	Masoretic Text
Ni.	Niphal
p.	page
pass.	passive
perf.	perfect
Pi.	Piel
pl.	plural
pp.	pages
ptc.	participle
Pu.	Pual
sfx.	suffix
sg.	singular
translit.	transliteration
V	any vowel
v	verse
vv	verses

Lesson 1

In This Lesson

1. The Alphabet
2. The Writing
3. The *Dāḡēš*
4. The *Bĕḡaḏkĕp̄aṯ* Letters

Terms to Know

bĕḡaḏkĕp̄aṯ
dāḡēš
spirant
stop
transliteration

Tip

Learning the Hebrew alphabet is a top priority, and you will do well to master the characters before moving ahead in this book. Write out the alphabet several times, then move on to the other exercises at the end of the chapter.

Answer Key

1.b.

1. ישׂראל	6. נפתּלי	11. טוביהו
2. יעקב	7. נתן	12. מלאכי
3. מלכּיצדק	8. בּית לחם	13. יחזקאל
4. ירבעם	9. אסף	14. חגּי
5. אסתּר	10. עמוס	15. דּוד

1.c.

1. *yrwšlm*	4. *yṣḥq*	7. *ʾḥymlḵ*
2. *ʾḇrhm*	5. *rḥl*	8. *ṣywn*
3. *śrh*	6. *šmwʾl*	9. *ṣp̄wn*

10. *ḥḇrwn*
11. *zḵryh*
12. *šmʿwn*
13. *bnymyn*
14. *rḇqh*
15. *lḇnwn*

REVIEW THE CONCEPTS

It is important to remember that a number of the Hebrew letters look similar to many beginners (I.2.d, p. 2). Many of the following exercises use letters that are often confused with each other, so read carefully! Remember to use the appropriate form for final letters (I.2.c) and to use a *dāḡēš* when a consonant is doubled or a stop (I.3, p. 3).

Write the following in Hebrew

1. *ḥhykl*
2. *yššh*
3. *bynh*
4. *smkṯhw*
5. *tḇkynh*
6. *ʿṣr*
7. *ʾḏršh*
8. *mslh*
9. *yrdp̄k*
10. *ʿṣrṯyḵm*

Transliterate the following

11. זרות
12. שׁלם
13. סמוכים
14. שׁמשׁון
15. מלכּי־צדק
16. יבטח
17. דּרך
18. מראה
19. יסףּ
20. תּחת

Answers

1. חהיכל
   The ח is closed, but the ה is open.
2. ישׁסה
3. בּינה
4. סמכתהו
5. תּבכּינה
   The base of the ב extends to the right, but the base of the כ does not. The top and bottom of the כ extend further to the left than the top and bottom of the נ.

6. עצר
   The left stroke of the צ is lower than that of the ע, and the left stroke of the צ is straight, while that of the ע is rounded.

7. אדרשׁה
   The ד is squared, while the ר is rounded.

8. מסלה

9. ירדּפך
   The ד is squared, while the ר is rounded. The final ך is squared and reaches below the line, while the ד and the ר are on the line.

10. עצרתיכם
    The left stroke of the צ is lower than that of the ע, and the left stroke of the צ is straight, while that of the ע is rounded.

11. *zrwṯ*
    The top of the ו extends only to the left, while the top of the ז extends to both sides.

12. *šlm*

13. *smwḵym*
    The ס is rounded, but the final ם is squared at the lower right-hand corner. The ו extends to the line, but the י is in the air.

14. *šmšwn*

15. *mlky-ṣdq*

16. *ybṭḥ*

17. *drḵ*
    The ד is squared, while the ר is rounded. The final ך is squared and reaches below the line, while the ד and the ר are on the line.

18. *mrʾh*

19. *ysp̄*

20. *tḥṯ*
    The left stroke of the ת has a small mark that is not found in the ח. The right stroke of the ת is rounded. while the right stroke of the ח is straight.

LESSON 2

IN THIS LESSON

1. Syllables
2. The Simple Vowels
3. The *Matres Lectionis*
4. Full and Defective Spelling
5. Stress
6. The *Šĕwāʾ*
7. The Composite *Šĕwāʾ*
8. Stops vs. Spirants
9. The *Qā́meṣ Ḥāṭûp̄*
10. The Furtive *Páṯaḥ*
11. The Quiescent *ʾĀ́lep̄*
12. Syllabification

TERMS TO KNOW

mappîq
matres lectionis
šĕwāʾ (vocal, composite, silent)
stress (ultima, penultima)
syllable (open/closed, stressed/unstressed, tonic/pretonic/propretonic)
vowel class (*a, i,* and *u*)

TIPS

1. Do not attempt to memorize all of the details in this lesson! This information will be reinforced by diligent attention to the exercises and the Review the Concepts section.

2. Master the ability to write transliteration into Hebrew and Hebrew into transliteration. The ability to do this on sight will be a tremendous aid throughout the learning process.

3. A short vowel in an open, unstressed syllable and a long vowel in a closed, unstressed syllable are unacceptable in Hebrew (II.12, p. 13).

4. When **א** appears to close a syllable, it quiesces, it is not vocalized, and the syllable functions as an open syllable (II.11, p. 13).

ANSWER KEY

2.a.

1. אִשָׁה
The ה-*mater* with *qā́meṣ* is transliterated as *ā(h)* (II.3.b, p. 7).

2. חָכְמָה
The ָ is *qāmeṣ ḥāṭûp̄* in a closed, unaccented syllable (II.9.a, p. 12). A closed syllable that does not end the word will take a silent *šĕwāʾ*.

3. שֵׁמוֹת
The *ḥṓlem-wāw* is transliterated as *ô* (II.3.b, p. 7).

4. תְהִלִים
The vocal *šĕwāʾ* is transliterated as *ĕ* (II.6, p. 9). When one sees *ĕ* in transliteration, it may be a vocal *šĕwāʾ* or a *ḥā́ṭep̄-sĕḡōl.* Assume it is a vocal *šĕwāʾ* unless it is with a guttural. The *ḥî́req-yōḏ* is transliterated as *î* (II.3.b, p. 7).

5. גָבוֹהַ
The furtive *pá̄ṯaḥ* is transliterated as (*a*) before the guttural (II.10, p. 12).

6. אִישָׁהּ
A dot called the *mappîq* is placed in the ה at the end of a word when the ה is a consonant and not a *mater* (II.3, note iv, p. 8).

7. יְהוּדָה

8. אַהֲרֹן
Gutturals prefer a composite *šĕwāʾ*. In this case, the composite *šĕwāʾ* is technically silent and is transliterated as (*a*) after the guttural (II.7, pp. 10–11).

9. לִוְיָתָן

10. שְׂדֵה
The ה-*mater* with *ṣērê* is transliterated as *ē(h)* (II.3.b, p. 7).

11. מִזְבֵחַ

12. מַאֲכָל

13. כְרֻבִים

14. מַלְאָכִי

15. בָעֳנִי
Before ֳ, ָ is always *qā́meṣ ḥāṭûp̄* (II.9.b, p. 12).

2.b.

1. *ʾăḏāmā(h)*—ground
   The ה-mater with *qā́meṣ* is transliterated as *ā(h)* (II.3.b, p. 7).
2. *ḥāḏāš*—new
3. *bĕrîṯ*—covenant
   A *šĕwāʾ* at the beginning of a word is vocal; the vocal *šĕwāʾ* is transliterated as *ĕ* (II.6, p. 9). The *ḥî́req-yōḏ* is transliterated as *î* (II.3.b, p. 7).
4. *ʿôlām*—eternity
5. *késep̄*—silver
   In transliteration, stress is represented by ´ (II.5, p. 8).
6. *nāḇîʾ*—prophet
7. *kōhēn*—priest
8. *ḥṓḏeš*—new moon, month
9. *dāḇār*—speech, word
10. *qôl*—voice, sound
    The *ḥṓlem-wāw* is transliterated as *ô* (II.3.b, p. 7).
11. *zāhāḇ*—gold
12. *gôy*—nation

2.c.

miš-lê šĕ-lō-mō(h) ḇen-dā-wīḏ mé-leḵ yiś-rā-ʾēl

lā-ḏá-ʿaṯ ḥoḵ-mā(h) û-mû-sār lĕ-hā-ḇîn ʾim-rê ḇî-nā(h)

lā-qá-ḥaṯ mû-sar haś-kēl ṣé-ḏeq û-miš-pāṭ û-mê-šā-rîm

lā-ṯēṯ lip̄-ṯā(ʾ)-yīm ʿor-mā(h) lĕ-ná-ʿar dá-ʿaṯ û-mĕ-zim-mā(h)

REVIEW THE CONCEPTS

True/False

1. If a *šĕwāʾ* is at the beginning of a word, it is silent.
2. If a *šĕwāʾ* is the second of two (except at end of word), it is silent.
3. If a *šĕwāʾ* comes immediately after a long vowel, it is silent.
4. If a *šĕwāʾ* is the first of two, it is vocal.

5. If a *šĕwāʾ* comes immediately after a short vowel, it is vocal.
6. If a *šĕwāʾ* comes immediately after a doubled consonant, it is vocal.
7. If a *šĕwāʾ* comes at the end of a word, it is silent.
8. In a closed, unaccented syllable, ָ is almost always *qā́meṣ ḥāṭûp̄*.
9. Before ֳ, ָ is always *qā́meṣ*.
10. If the small *méṯeḡ* appears with the ָ, the vowel is always *qā́meṣ*.

Answers

1. false	6. true
2. false	7. true
3. false	8. true
4. false	9. false
5. false	10. true

Lesson 3

In This Lesson

1. The Noun: Gender and Number
   gender: masculine, feminine
   number: singular, plural, dual
2. Changes in Nouns with Endings
   reduction of vowels to *šĕwāʾ*
   contraction of *-áyi-* and *-ā́we-*

Terms to Know

contraction
gender
number
reduction
stress (II)
syllable (II)

Tips

1. The most common and important fs suffix is *-ā(h)*, as in סוּסָה "mare." Still, do not overlook the less common fs suffixes with final ת: *-ût* (אַלְמָנוּת), *-ît* (בְּרִית), *-et* (קְטֹ֫רֶת), *-at* (בַּת). See III.1.b, p. 17.

2. The rule for pretonic reduction (III.2.a.ii, p. 20) only applies to words that also have a propretonic syllable. Compare exercises III.a.6 (no reduction) and III.a.9 (reduction) in this regard.

3. The contraction rules in III.2.b.i-ii, p. 20, if learned now, will be helpful for understanding several future lessons. When *-áyi-* and *-ā́we-* lose their stress, they contract to *-ê-* and *-ô-*, respectively. Study the examples with care, and you will be amply rewarded in later chapters!

Answer Key

3.a.

1. שִׁירִים
2. תּוֹרוֹת
   The fs suffix is dropped prior to adding the fp suffix (III.1.d, p. 18).

3. אֲדוֹנִים
With propretonic reduction of original initial *qāmeṣ* (III.2.a.i, p. 20).

4. כּוֹכָבִים

5. יָדוֹת

6. אֵלִים
The rule at III.2.a.ii (p. 20) concerning reduction of pretonic syllable with *ṣērê* does not apply if there is no propretonic syllable. Thus, *ṣērê* is not reduced in this word.

7. לְבָבוֹת

8. חֲגָבִים

9. כֹּהֲנִים
With pretonic reduction of original *ṣērê* (III.2.a.ii, p. 20).

10. עֲנָבִים

11. זֵיתִים
With contraction of original *-áyi-* (III.2.b.i, p. 20).

12. אֹיְבִים

13. צַדִּיקִים

14. הֵיכָלוֹת
This form is an irregular mp with the fp ending (BDB הֵיכָל, p. 228). The propretonic syllable does not reduce and is always spelled with *ṣērê-yōḏ*. This is because הֵיכָל is not originally Hebrew, but a loanword (see IV Vocabulary, p. 36, n. 2); ordinarily, the propretonic *ṣērê* would be reduced to *šĕwāʾ*.

15. מַלְאָכִים

16. מִלְחָמוֹת

17. מִשְׁפָּחוֹת

18. מִנְחוֹת

3.b.

1. פָּנִים

2. יָדַיִם

3. מַמְלָכוֹת

4. אָזְנַיִם

See the vocabulary list in this chapter. The initial vowel is *qāmeṣ ḥāṭûp̄* (II.9.a, p. 12).

5. נְבִיאִים
6. שָׁמַ֫יִם
7. כֹּהֲנִים
8. אִמּוֹת
   See the vocabulary list in this chapter.
9. גּוֹיִם/גּוֹיִים
   The latter (defective) spelling is the more frequently attested: *gôyīm*. For the rarer, full spelling, see Gen 25:23; Ps 79:10 (BDB גּוֹי, p. 156).
10. עֵינַ֫יִם
11. מִשְׁפָּטִים
12. שֹׁפְטִים

Review the Concepts

1. Hebrew nouns may be masculine or ___________ in gender, and they may be singular, dual, or plural in ___________ (III.1, p. 17).
2. True or false: Most feminine nouns show either a ה or ת at the end (III.1.b, p. 17).
3. Circle one: Masculine plural nouns are normally marked by the ending (ִים - or ַ֫יִם - or וֹת) (III.1.c, p. 18).
4. Circle one: When adding a suffix to a word, if the suffixed word has a propretonic syllable and if it is not reduced, then in the pretonic syllable (*ṣērê* or *qā́meṣ* or *ḥṓlem*) is reduced to *šĕwāʾ* (III.2.a.ii, p 20).
5. Nouns with stressed *-ā́we-* contract predictably when suffixes are added. What is the plural of the masculine noun מָ֫וֶת?

Answers

1. feminine, number
2. true
3. ִים -
4. *ṣērê*
5. מוֹתִים

Lesson 4

In This Lesson

1. Hebrew Roots and Word Patterns
2. Weak Radicals: see summary (IV, p. 35)
3. Nouns with Prefixes: -מ, -ת, -א

Terms to Know

compensatory lengthening
diphthong
radical
virtual doubling
vowel lengthening

Tips

1. The model root קטל (*qṭl*) is used to discuss word patterns in Hebrew. In various word patterns, the ק represents the first radical, the ט represents the second radical, and the ל represents the third radical of the root.

2. Master the concepts of compensatory lengthening and virtual doubling, since they apply not only to noun patterns but also to all Hebrew words. Compensatory lengthening and virtual doubling describe what happens when one expects a radical to be doubled (based on a Hebrew word pattern) but the radical is not doubled because it is a guttural or ר.

(a) With compensatory lengthening, the vowel before the guttural lengthens (*a* to *ā; i* to *ē; u* to *ō*).

(b) With virtual doubling, the vowel before the guttural is unchanged.

3. When identifying Hebrew roots of nouns, there is no precise formula to follow; often one must consider several possibilities and consult a dictionary. It helps, however, to become familiar with the following features.

(a) If -מ, -ת, or -א begins a word, this letter may be a prefix.

(b) A *dāgēš* may indicate that a נ has been assimilated.

(c) A ָה - may be the fs suffix.

(d) Any noun ending in ֶה - has a root ending in ה.

(e) A י or ו may indicate several possibilities: (1) at the beginning of a word, roots that originally began with ו are listed as beginning with י; (2) in a noninitial position, י or ו may appear as a *mater;* (3) at the end of a word, י or ו appear as a final ה.

ANSWER KEY

4.a.

1. *qōṭēl*
2. *qaṭṭāl*
3. *qāṭēl*
4. *qiṭṭēl*
5. *qāṭōl*
6. *qaṭṭāl*
7. *qāṭēl*
8. *qiṭṭēl*
9. *qaṭṭāl*
10. *qāṭēl*
11. *qōṭēl*
12. *qāṭōl*
13. *miqṭāl*
14. *qōṭēl*
15. *miqṭāl*
16. *qāṭōl*
17. *miqṭāl*
18. *qiṭṭēl*

4.b.

1. כוס
2. בצר
   The מ is a prefix (IV.3.a, pp. 32–33). When finding the root of any word beginning with מ, ת, or א, begin by determining if this letter is a prefix.
3. כון
4. קנה
   Remember that any noun ending in הֶ - has a root ending in ה (IV.2.c.vii.α, pp. 30–31).
5. נשׂא
   The מ is a prefix (IV.3.a, pp. 32–33), and the *dāḡēš* in the שּׂ indicates that a נ was assimilated into the שׂ (IV.2.b, p. 27).
6. ערה
   The final הָ - of עֶרְוָה is the feminine singular noun ending (III.2.c, p. 20 and IV.2.c.vii.α, pp. 30–31). This leaves us, then, with ערו. Words originally ending with ו or י appear in the dictionary as III-*Hē* (IV.2.c.vii, p. 30), so the root is ערה.
7. ירא
   The מ of מורא is a prefix, leaving us with ורא. In the dictionaries, roots that originally began with ו are listed as beginning with י (IV.2.c.i, pp. 27–28).
8. בין
9. חצה
   Words originally ending with ו or י appear in the dictionary with a final ה (IV.2.c.vii, p. 30).

10. יעד
The מ of מועד is a prefix, leaving us with ועד. In the dictionaries, roots that originally began with ו are listed as beginning with י (IV.2.c.i, pp. 27–28).

11. אור
The ו is a *mater,* but it indicates a root with ו as the second radical (IV.2.c.v, p. 29).

12. צור
The final ָה - is the feminine singular noun ending (III.2.c, p. 20 and IV.2.c.vii.*α*, pp. 30–31). Regarding the second radical, II-*Wāw* and II-*Yōḏ* roots are not always distinguished (IV.2.c.v, p. 29).

13. קיץ
The root is II-*Yōḏ,* and the original **ay* becomes *-áyi* when stressed, as in קַ֫יִץ (IV.2.c.iv.*α*, pp. 28–29).

14. נצב
The מ is a prefix (IV.3.a, p. 32–33), and the *dāḡēš* in the צ indicates that a נ was assimilated into the צ (IV.2.b, p. 27).

15. זרח
The א is a prefix (IV.3.c, p. 34).

16. רום
The final ָה - is the feminine singular noun ending (III.2.c, p. 20 and IV.2.c.vii.a, pp. 30–31), and the ת is a prefix (IV.3.b, pp. 33–34).

17. ידה
ת is a prefix (IV.3.b, pp. 33–34), and initial ו is listed as י in the dictionary. The III-*Hē* has dropped off before the addition of the fs noun suffix ָה -.

18. רעה

4.c.

1. דְּבָרִים
2. רוּחוֹת
3. אֵילִים
4. אוֹרִים
5. אֲבָנִים
6. עֲינוֹת

7. עֲוֹנוֹת
8. מִלְחָמוֹת
9. אֲרֹנִים
10. הֵיכָלוֹת

    This form is an irregular mp with the fp ending (BDB, p. 228). The propretonic syllable has an irreducibly long vowel; הֵיכָל is a loanword (Vocabulary IV, p. 36, n. 2).

11. מַלְאָכִים
12. עוֹלוֹת
13. יָדִים
14. יָדוֹת
15. מְקוֹמוֹת

REVIEW THE CONCEPTS

1. Hebrew roots are made up of how many radicals (consonants)?
2. What is wrong with the following word in the *qaṭṭāl* pattern? פַּרָשׁ
3. What does the *dāḡēš* in the ט indicate in the following word? מַטֶּה
4. The following word is of the *měqaṭṭēl* pattern: מְשַׁלֵּחַ. How do you account for the final vowel?
5. What is wrong with the following word: עְבָדִים?

Answers

1. Three.
2. Gutturals and the letter ר cannot be doubled by the *dāḡēš,* so here the vowel just before the ר (or a guttural) becomes long through compensatory lengthening. The correct form of this word is פָּרָשׁ.
3. It indicates that a נ was assimilated into the ט. The root of this word is נטה.
4. The reason for the furtive *páṯaḥ* is that the form ends with ח, a guttural. Gutturals prefer *a*-class vowels.
5. Gutturals prefer the composite *šěwāʾ* rather than the simple vocal *šěwāʾ*. The correct form of the word is thus עֲבָדִים.

Lesson 5 and Excursus A

In This Lesson

1. Geminate Nouns
2. Segolate Nouns
3. Irregular Plurals

Terms to Know

compensatory lengthening (IV)
gemination
penultima (II)
root (IV)
virtual doubling (II)
vowel class (*a*, *i*, and *u*) (II)
word patterns (IV)

Tips

1. Geminate nouns have identical second and third consonants. There are three types of geminate nouns, corresponding to the three vowel classes: *a*-type (**qall*); *i*-type (**qill*); *u*-type (**qull*).

2. Segolate nouns are two-syllable nouns with stress on the penultima. Singular segolates are generally marked by *sĕḡōls* (sometimes *páṯaḥs* with gutturals). There are three types of segolate nouns, corresponding to the three vowel classes: *a*-type (**qaṭl*); *i*-type (**qiṭl*); *u*-type (**qoṭl* [originally **quṭl*]).

3. Segolate plural nouns follow the pattern *qĕṭālîm* or *qĕṭālôṯ* (V.2, p. 41).

4. Keep in mind the list of irregular plurals; it contains many common nouns (V.3, p. 43).

Answer Key

5.a.

1. פָּרִים
   Since the ר cannot take a *dāḡēš*, compensatory lengthening occurs (V.1.a, p. 38).

2. תֻּפִּים

Since gemination is marked by the strong *dāḡēš*, the original *u*-vowel is retained in the plural; it lengthens to *ō* in the singular when gemination is not marked (V.1.c, note, p. 39).

3. צֻרִים

4. קִנִּים

Since gemination is marked by the strong *dāḡēš*, the original *i*-vowel is retained in the plural; it lengthens to *ē* in the singular when gemination is not marked (V.1.b, note i, p. 39).

5. סֻכּוֹת

6. שָׂרִים

7. חֻקִּים

8. פִּנּוֹת

When the feminine suffix ה, - is added to the singular form, gemination can be marked by the strong *dāḡēš*, and the original vowel is retained.

9. חִצִּים

10. דֻּבִּים

11. הָרִים

12. אָמּוֹת

13. כָּרִים

14. עַמִּים

15. תֻּמִּים

5.b.

Several nouns in this exercise have irregular plurals. Take special note of the list on page 43.

1. מְלָכִים

Segolate plural nouns have the pattern *qĕṭālîm* or *qĕṭālôṯ* (V.2, p. 41).

2. בָּנִים

3. אַחִים

4. עָרִים

5. בָּנוֹת

6. יָמִים

7. אָבוֹת

8. עֲבָדִים
Gutturals prefer a composite *šěwāʾ* (IV.2.a.ii, pp. 26–27).

9. קֳדָשִׁים
Segolates of the **qoṭl* type take the plural pattern *qŏṭālîm* or *qŏṭālôṯ* (V.2.c, note ii, p. 42).

10. נְפָשׁוֹת

11. יַמִּים

12. רָאשִׁים

13. אֲנָשִׁים

14. כֵּלִים
See the vocabulary list on page 44.

15. דְּרָכִים

16. בָּתִּים
This is an irregular plural (V.3, p. 43).

17. אֲרָצוֹת

18. מַעֲשִׂים

19. חֳדָשִׁים

20. נָשִׁים

21. אֳהָלִים

Review the Concepts

Give the plural for the following forms.

1. בֹּ֫קֶר
2. קֶ֫רֶב
3. נַ֫עַר
4. נֶ֫דֶר
5. עֵ֫דֶר
6. שַׂק
7. פַּח
8. מְסִלָּה
9. תְּפִלָּה
10. אֵם

Answers

1. בְּקָרִים
2. קְבָרִים
3. נְעָרִים
   For the singular form, a guttural may draw a *páṯaḥ* in the second syllable or in both syllables (V.2.a, note, p. 41).
4. נְדָרִים
5. עֲדָרִים
6. שַׂקִּים
7. פַּחִים
8. מְסִלּוֹת
   Nouns with geminate roots may have prefixes (V.1.d, pp. 39–40).
9. תְּפִלּוֹת
10. אִמּוֹת

Excursus A Answer Key

	Word	Root	BDB page for root and the derived word
1.	תְּשׁוּבָה	שׁוב	996, 1000
2.	מִרְעֶה	רעה	944, 945
3.	מַסַּע	נסע	652
4.	מִזְמֹר	זמר	274
5.	אֵיתָנִים	יתן	450
6.	שָׂפָה	שׂפה	973
7.	מַבָּט	נבט	613
8.	דֹּב	דבב	179
9.	מַכָּה	נכה	645, 646
10.	מֵאָה	מאה	547
11.	מֵיתָר	יתר	451, 452
12.	תְּהִלָּה	הלל	237, 239

13. קִינָה	קין	883, 884
14. מַגֵּפָה	נגף	619, 620
15. גַּאֲוָה	גאה	144
16. מוֹרֶה	ירה	434, 435
17. חֲנִית	חנה	333
18. שְׁפִי	שׁפה	1045, 1046
19. גֵּרִים	גור	157, 158 (see *GBH* IV.2.c.vi, p. 30)
20. צָרִים	צרר	865
21. מוֹלֶ֫דֶת	ילד	408, 409
22. תּוֹלֵדוֹת	ילד	408, 410
23. מֶמְשָׁלָה	משׁל	605, 606
24. מַעֲשִׂים	עשׂה	793, 795
25. מַחֲשָׁבָה	חשׁב	362, 364
26. מַרְאֶה	ראה	906, 909
27. מְנוֹרָה	נור	632, 633
28. שָׂרָה	שׂרר/שׂרה	975/977, 979
29. עֵת	ענה	772, 773 (see *GBH* V.1.b, note ii, p. 39)
30. פָּרָה	פרר/פרה	826/830, 831

REVIEW THE CONCEPTS

For additional practice with BDB, find the nouns listed in 5.a and 5.b and give the BDB page number for each.

Answers

5.a.

1. פַּר (830)
2. תֹּף (1074)
3. צַר (865)
4. קֵן (890)
5. סֶפָח (697)
6. שַׂר (978)
7. חֹק (349)
8. פִּנָּה (819)
9. חֵץ (346)
10. דֹּב (179)
11. הַר (249)
12. אַמָּה (52)
13. כַּר (503)
14. עַם (766)
15. תֹּם (1070)

5.b.

1. מֶ֫לֶךְ (572)
2. בֵּן (119)
3. אָח (26)
4. עִיר (746)
5. בַּת (123; see *GBH*, Excursus A, pp. 50–51)
6. יוֹם (398)
7. אָב (3)
8. עֶ֫בֶד (713)
9. קֹ֫דֶשׁ (871)
10. נֶ֫פֶשׁ (659)
11. יָם (410)
12. רֹאשׁ (910)
13. אִישׁ (35)
14. כְּלִי (479)
15. דֶּ֫רֶךְ (202)
16. בַּ֫יִת (108)
17. אֶ֫רֶץ (75)
18. מַעֲשֶׂה (795)
19. חֹ֫דֶשׁ (294)
20. אִשָּׁה (61)
21. אֹ֫הֶל (13)

Lesson 6

In This Lesson

1. The Definite Article: -· הַ, -הָ, -הַ, -הֶ
2. Prefixed Prepositions: בְּ, כְּ, לְ
3. The Rule of *Šĕwāʾ*
4. Other Prepositions: אַחַר, לִפְנֵי, תַּחַת, נֶגֶד
5. The Preposition מִן: independent and prefixed forms
6. The Conjunction ו
7. Loss of the Strong *Dāḡēš* (see tip 3, below, on "Sqnmlwy").
8. The Verbless Clause

Terms to Know

compensatory lengthening (IV)
composite *šĕwāʾ* (II)
conjunction
definite article
gutturals (א, ה, ח, ע) (II)
preposition
verbless clause
virtual doubling (IV)

Tips

1. Remember that virtual doubling is not a mysterious concept but is a shorthand term for the long-winded phrase, "In lieu of doubling, one expects compensatory lengthening of the vowel preceding this guttural (or ר) but does not find it." When a form calls for doubling of a consonant but that consonant is a guttural or ר, compensatory lengthening or virtual doubling is required by syllabification rules, which do not permit a short vowel in an open, unstressed syllable (II.12, p. 13). Review IV.2.a.i, p. 26.

2. A handy mnemonic for recalling when the conjunction ו becomes a *šûreq* וּ (VI.6.b–c, p. 58) is "BuMP *Šĕmûʾēl*": that is, before words beginning with בּ, מ, or פּ, and also before words with initial simple vocal *šĕwāʾ*.

3. A handy mnemonic for recalling the consonants from VI.7 (p. 59) is "Sqnmlwy" /squeen-muh-lay-wee/, where uppercase S stands for "any sibilant." Remember that this phenomenon is not a "rule": though the strong

dāḡēš will often be lost in these letters when taking a *šĕwāʾ*, the *dāḡēš* may be unpredictably retained.

ANSWER KEY

6.a.

1. הַלַּ֫יְלָה
2. הָעִיר
   With compensatory lengthing in the definite article (VI.1.b.i, p. 54).
3. הֶעָרִים
   For this plural form, see Irregular Plurals, V.3, p. 43. For *sĕḡōl* under the definite article, see VI.1.b.iii, p. 54.
4. הָאָב
5. הַהֵיכָל
   With virtual doubling in the definite article (VI.1.b.ii, p. 54).
6. הַחַטָּאת
7. הָעָם
8. הָאָ֫רֶץ
9. הָאֵילִים
10. הָעֲוֹנוֹת
    It should be clear that the first ו is a consonant, not a *mater*: the ע already takes a *šĕwāʾ* and thus cannot also be followed by a *ḥṓlem* (II.1.b, p. 5).
11. הֶהָרִים
    Although the definite singular form is הָהָר (VI.1.c, p. 55), the definite plural form is הֶהָרִים (VI.1.b.iii, p. 54).
12. הָרָאשִׁים
13. הַחֲרָבוֹת
14. הַכֵּלִים
15. הַנָּשִׁים

6.b.

1. אַחַר/אַחֲרֵי הָרוּחַ
2. מֵהָאָ֫רֶץ/מִן־הָאָ֫רֶץ
   The preposition מִן may be independent or prefixed (VI.5, pp. 57–58).

3. וּבֶעָרִים
Note that the *šûreq* results from "BuMP *Šĕmû'ēl*" (tip 2, above; VI.6.b–c, p. 58). The *sĕgōl* points to a definite article "hidden" behind the preposition בּ (VI.2.b, pp. 55–56).

4. בִּבְרִית

5. בָּאֳהָלִים
The initial vowel is *qámeṣ ḥāṭûp̄* (VI.3.b, p. 56). For the plural form of this **qoṭl* segolate אֹ֫הֶל, see V.2.c, p. 42.

6. כֵּאלֹהִים
For quiescence of the א and the initial *ṣērê*, see II.11, p. 13, and VI.3.b, p. 56.

7. תַּ֫חַת דָּוִיד הַמֶּ֫לֶךְ

8. נָבִיא לַגּוֹיִם

9. בַּיּוֹם וּבַלַּ֫יְלָה

10. בֵּין הַחֹ֫שֶׁךְ וּבֵין הָאוֹר

11. מִשָּׁ֫מַיִם עַד־אֶ֫רֶץ

12. מֵהָאֲנָשִׁים
For the translation "some of," see VI.5, pp. 57–58; this use of מִן will receive more attention in lesson VII.

6.c.

1. the silver and the gold
2. princes and slaves
3. face to face
4. before the mountain
5. like the people, like the priest (or, "people and priest alike")
6. from army to army
7. a hand for ("in place of") a hand, a foot for a foot
For translation of this preposition, review VI Vocabulary, p. 60.
8. from day until night
9. the water under the heaven (or, "under the sky")
Note the "compound preposition" (see note to VI Vocabulary, p. 60).
10. in Judah and in Jerusalem
For the initial vowels, see Rule of *Šĕwā'* (VI.3.a, p. 56).
11. darkness to light and light to darkness
12. between the day and the night

6.d. Gen 1:1–6

v 1: בְּרֵאשִׁית Translating this first word in the Hebrew Bible is notoriously difficult; for now, simply translate it traditionally: "In the beginning. . ."—בָּרָא "(subject: God) created"—וְאֵת . . . אֵת untranslated markers of the definite object of the verb (בָּרָא).

v 2: הָיְתָה "was"—וְרוּחַ אֱלֹהִים "and the wind/spirit of God"—מְרַחֶפֶת "was hovering/swooping."

v 3: וַיֹּאמֶר "and (subject) said"—יְהִי "let there be"—וַיְהִי "and there was."

v 4: וַיַּרְא "and (subject) saw"—כִּי־טוֹב "that it was good"—וַיַּבְדֵּל "and (subject) made a separation."

v 5: וַיִּקְרָא "and (subject) called"—לָאוֹר "(with reference to) the light"—קָרָא "he called."

v. 6: בְּתוֹךְ "in the midst of"—וִיהִי "and let there be"—מַבְדִּיל "a distinction/separation"—To translate בֵּין מַיִם לָמָיִם, consult BDB בַּיִן 1.b, p. 107.

Review the Concepts

1. Where a guttural "should" be doubled by addition of the definite article, one finds instead compensatory ____________ or ____________ doubling.

2. Complete this exercise: הַמֶּלֶךְ + לְ > ________, "for the king."

3. If, at the beginning of a word, a simple vocal *šĕwāʾ* is followed by a composite *šĕwāʾ*, the former becomes the corresponding ________ vowel of the composite *šĕwāʾ*. Thus, חֲלוֹם + בְּ > _________ "in a dream."

4. What is "BuMP *Šĕmûʾēl*"?

5. What is "Sqnmlwy"?

Answers

1. lengthening; virtual

2. לַמֶּלֶךְ

3. short; בַּחֲלוֹם

4. A memory tip illustrating the use of *šûreq* for the conjunction וּ.

5. A memory tip for illustrating the loss of strong *dāgēš* in some consonants when followed by *šĕwāʾ*.

Lesson 7

In This Lesson

1. The Inflection of the Adjective: gender and number
2. Adjectival Patterns: *qāṭōl, qāṭēl, qāṭāl, qall,* etc.
3. Uses of the Adjective: attributive, predicate, substantive
4. Agreement of the Adjective with the Noun: agreement with lexical gender rather than with form
5. Special Uses of מִן: comparative, partitive
6. The Adjective with מְאֹד: "very," "exceedingly"
7. Nouns in Apposition

Terms to Know

apposition
attributive adjective
comparative
partitive
predicate adjective
substantive

Tips

1. Keep in mind that the adjective agrees with the noun in its lexical gender rather than its form (i.e., הָאָ֫רֶץ הַטּוֹבָה ["the good land"]—the adjective טוֹב is in the feminine form since the noun אֶ֫רֶץ is feminine).

2. For the attributive adjective, remember that it:
   (a) modifies a noun;
   (b) comes after the noun in Hebrew;
   (c) agrees with the noun in gender, number, and definiteness (and may take the definite article).

3. For the predicate adjective, remember that it:
   (a) describes the state of the noun;
   (b) may come before or after the noun;
   (c) agrees in gender and number with the noun but never takes the definite article.

4. Remember AAA (*attributive* comes *after* and *agrees*) but PPP (*predicative prefers* to *precede*).

ANSWER KEY

7.a.

1. גּוֹי קָדוֹשׁ
2. מֶ֫לֶךְ חָדָשׁ
3. עִיר קְטַנָּה
   Remember that the adjective agrees with the noun in its lexical gender rather than its form (VII.4.a, p. 73).
4. רוּחַ רָעָה
5. חָכְמָה גְּדוֹלָה
6. עָרִים רַבּוֹת
7. אֲבָנִים יְקָרוֹת
8. רָעָב בָּעִיר
9. הַדָּבָר טוֹב מְאֹד or טוֹב מְאֹד הַדָּבָר
10. הַמֶּ֫לֶךְ זָקֵן מְאֹד or זָקֵן מְאֹד הַמֶּ֫לֶךְ
11. הַדָּבָר הָרָשָׁע
12. כַּצַּדִּיק כָּרָשָׁע

7.b.

1. to another man
2. the living God
   אֱלֹהִים is not marked as definite with an article, but אֱלֹהִים is a unique appellative that is "inherently definite" (see *IBHS,* 13.4b, p. 240; for more on *IBHS* and reference grammars generally, see Excursus D).
3. to another land
4. a large and numerous people
   While the form of the conjunction as וָ with רַב does not correspond precisely to the rules learned in VI.6, pp. 58–59, this vocalization does occur with certain pairs of words or when the conjunction is immediately before certain accented syllables, such as תֹהוּ וָבֹ֫הוּ in Gen 1:2 (see BDB, p. 251; Joüon, §104c, d, pp. 347–49).
5. bread for the hungry
6. the righteous and the wicked alike

7. and the famine was severe (heavy) in the land
8. the man Moses was very great
9. better than sons and (better than) daughters
10. the new heavens and the new earth
11. many nations and great kings
12. the good were very good, and the bad were very bad

7.c. Gen 1:14–19

v 14: וַיֹּאמֶר "(subject) said"—יְהִי "let there be"—מְאֹרֹת (defective spelling for מְאוֹרוֹת)—בִּרְקִיעַ "in the expanse of"—לְהַבְדִּיל "to separate"—וְהָיוּ "so that they shall be"—לְאֹתֹת "for signs"— וּלְמוֹעֲדִים "and for seasons"—וְשָׁנִים irreg. fp of שָׁנָה.

v 15: לְהָאִיר "to shine"—וַיְהִי־כֵן "and it was so."

v 16: וַיַּעַשׂ "and (subject) made"—אֶת־שְׁנֵי "the two" (אֶת־ is an untranslatable marker of the definite object)—לְמֶמְשֶׁלֶת "for dominion of."

v 17: וַיִּתֵּן אֹתָם "and (subject) put them."

v 18: וְלִמְשֹׁל "and to dominate" (object indicated by the preposition בְּ)—וַיַּרְא "and (subject) saw"—כִּי־טוֹב "that it was good."

v 19: וַיְהִי "it was."

REVIEW THE CONCEPTS

Translate the following phrases and indicate whether the adjective is used attributively, predicatively, or substantively.

1. זְקֵנִים הָאֲנָשִׁים
2. צַדִּיקִים בָּאָרֶץ
3. גְּדוֹלָה הָאֶבֶן
4. אִשָּׁה יָפָה
5. נֶפֶשׁ יְקָרָה
6. טוֹב־וְיָשָׁר יְהוָה

Translate the following phrases and indicate whether מִן has a comparative or partitive use.

7. מִן־הָעָם בִּיהוּדָה
8. טוֹב מִמֶּלֶךְ

9. יָקָר מִזָּהָב
10. מִן־הַנְּבִיאִים

Answers

1. the men are old: predicative
2. righteous ones are in the land: substantive
3. the stone is great: predicative
4. a beautiful woman *or* a woman is beautiful: attributive or predicative
5. a precious life *or* life is precious: attributive or predicative
6. good and upright is YHWH: predicative
7. some of the people in Judah: partitive
8. better than a king: comparative
9. more precious than gold: comparative
10. some of the prophets: partitive

Lesson 8

In This Lesson

1. The Verbal Patterns: seven major verbal patterns
2. The Inflection of the Participle
3. The Qal Active Participle: strong verb קֹטֵל; weak roots
4. Uses of the Participle
5. The Qal Passive Participle: strong verb קָטוּל; weak roots

Terms to Know

attributive adjective (VII)
definiteness (VI)
gender (III)
inflection
number (III)
parse
predicate adjective (VII)
substantive (VII)
verbal adjective
verbal patterns

Tips

1. The pattern of the Qal active participle is *qōṭēl*. For most root types, look for the *ḥōlem* with the first consonant as a marker of the Qal active participle. Use the synopsis on page 81 as a learning aid.

2. The pattern of the Qal passive participle is *qāṭûl*. Look for the *šûreq* with the second consonant as a marker of the Qal passive participle. Use the synopsis on page 84 as a learning aid.

3. The participle may function:

(a) predicatively (agrees with noun in gender and number; does not take article);

(b) attributively (agrees with noun in gender, number, and definiteness and comes after the noun; may translate with relative pronoun "who");

(c) substantively (as a noun).

Answer Key

8.a.

1. Qal act. ptc. ms נָתַן to give
2. Qal act. ptc. fs יָצָא to go out, go forth
   In the Qal act. fs participle of III-*ʾĀlep̄* roots, the א quiesces and the second syllable takes a long vowel (VIII.3.d, p. 80).
3. Qal act. ptc. mp עָלָה to go up, ascend
   In the Qal act. mp and fp participle of III-*Hē* roots, the weak radical drops and the plural endings are added (VIII.3.e, p. 80).
4. Qal act. ptc. ms עָשָׂה to make, do
   The Qal act. ms participle of III-*Hē* roots ends in ה ֶ - (VIII.3.e, p. 80; cf. IV.2.c.vii.a, p. 30).
5. Qal act. ptc. fs בּוֹא to come, enter
   Qal act. participles of II-*Wāw/ Yōḏ* roots do not retain the middle radical and do not follow the normal *qōṭēl* pattern (VIII.3.f, pp. 80–81).
6. Qal pass. ptc. fs אָהַב to love
7. Qal act. ptc. mp אָמַר to say
8. Qal act. ptc. fs עָמַד to stand, remain
9. Qal pass. ptc. ms נָטָה to stretch out, extend, incline
   Qal pass. participles of III-*Hē* roots have י as the third radical (VIII.5.b, note i, p. 84).
10. Qal act. ptc. fs קָרָא to call
11. Qal pass. ptc. mp כָּתַב to write
12. Qal act. ptc. fs יָדַע to know
    Gutturals prefer *a*-class vowels (VIII.3.c, p. 80).
13. Qal pass. ptc. fs עָשָׂה to make, do
    Qal pass. participles of III-*Hē* roots have י as the third radical (VIII.5.b, note i, p. 84).
14. Qal act. ptc. mp מָצָא to find
15. Qal pass. ptc. fs בָּנָה to build

8.b.

1. Qal act. ptc. fp כָּרַע to bow down, bend
2. Qal act. ptc. ms סָבַב to go around

3. Qal act. ptc. ms צוּם to fast
   Qal act. participles of II-*Wāw/ Yōḏ* roots do not retain the middle radical nor follow the normal *qōṭēl* pattern (VIII.3.f, pp. 80–81).

4. Qal act. ptc. fs אָפָה to bake
   The Qal act. fs participle of III-*Hē* roots ends in ָה - (VIII.3.e, p. 80).

5. Qal act. ptc. mp גָּאַל to redeem
   Gutturals prefer composite *šěwā'* (VIII.3.b, p. 79).

6. Qal act. ptc. ms שׁוּב to return

7. Qal act. ptc. mp שָׁדַד to plunder, destroy

8. Qal act. ptc. fs נָפַל to fall

9. Qal act. ptc. fs שִׂים to put

10. Qal act. ptc. ms כָּרַת to cut

11. Qal act. ptc. mp אָפָה to bake

12. Qal act. ptc. ms נוּס to flee

13. Qal act. ptc. mp שׁוּב to return

14. Qal act. ptc. ms רוּם to be high, exalted

15. Qal act. ptc. fs בָּכָה to weep
    See VIII.3.e, note, p. 80.

8.c.

1. הַיֹּלֶדֶת
2. הַנֹּטֶה הַשָּׁמַ֫יִם
3. הַכְּתוּבִים
4. הַיֹּשְׁבִים בִּיהוּדָה
5. בְּיָד נְטוּיָה
6. יְרוּשָׁלַ֫ם הַבְּנוּיָה כְּעִיר (see Ps 122:3)
   For the spelling of "Jerusalem," see III.1.e, p. 19, n. 2. The כ is a spirant because it is preceded by an open syllable (II.8.a, p. 11). In the identical phrase found in Ps 122:3 the כ is a stop; this is due to the presence of the *'aṯnāḥ* on the preceding open vowel (see GKC, §21.b, p. 53).
7. אִשָּׁה יֹדַ֫עַת אִישׁ
8. מַלְאָךְ אַחֵר יֹצֵא

9. הַכָּתוּב לְחַיִּים

10. הַכֵּלִים הָעֲשׂוּיִים

8.d.

1. YHWH is passing by.
2. YHWH loves justice.
3. the ones who were passing through the land
   On the translation of the participle here, see VIII.4.b, p. 83.
4. the people who were living in the land
5. a listening ear and a seeing eye
6. a man who loves wisdom
7. the people who were walking in (the) darkness
8. (ones) building a temple for YHWH
   For the translation of the participle here, see VIII.4.d, p. 84.
9. Disaster is about to go out from nation to nation.
   For this use of the participle, see VIII.4.a.iii, p. 82.
10. slaves on horses and princes walking like slaves on the earth

8.e. Ps 146:5–10

v 5: "How fortunate is the one whose help is the God of Jacob, whose help is in YHWH his God. . . . "

v 6: וְאֶת־ The אֶת is the untranslatable marker of the definite direct object —וְאֶת־כָּל־אֲשֶׁר־בָּם "and all that is in them."

v 7: מַתִּיר "one who sets free."

v 9: גֵּרִים This and the next few nouns should be treated as definite, even though the article is not present. The absence of the article in poetic Hebrew is not unusual (this will be explained in Excursus E)—יְעוֹדֵד "he supports"—וְדֶרֶךְ "and the way of"—יְעַוֵּת "he thwarts."

v 10: יִמְלֹךְ "(subject) shall reign"—אֱלֹהַיִךְ צִיּוֹן "your God, O Zion"—The *šĕwā'* is vocal in הַלְלוּ־יָהּ "praise Yah!"; see II.6.b.iii, p. 10, n. 2. (יָהּ is a shortened form of the divine name יהוה.)

Review the Concepts

Translate the following phrases, parse each participle, and identify the function of each participle.

1. אֱלֹהִים יֹדֵעַ
2. הָאֲנָשִׁים אֹמְרִים לַיהוָה
3. הַיֹּרְדִים אֶל־הַיָּם
4. קוֹל קֹרֵא בַּחֹשֶׁךְ
5. הַנָּשִׁים עֹלוֹת
6. מִשְׁפָּט כָּתוּב
7. הַדָּבָר כָּתוּב בַּסְּפָרִים
8. כַּכָּתוּב בַּתּוֹרָה
9. הָאִשָּׁה הַקֹּרֵאת בְּקוֹל גָּדוֹל
10. הָעָם הַיֹּצְאִים מוּלִים

Answers

1. God knows—Qal act. ptc. ms יָדַע to know; predicative
2. The men were speaking to YHWH—Qal act. ptc. mp אָמַר to say; predicative
3. The ones going down to the sea—Qal act. ptc. mp יָרַד to go down; substantive
4. A voice is calling in the darkness—Qal act. ptc. ms קָרָא to call; predicative
5. The women are going up—Qal act. ptc. fp עָלָה to go up; predicative
6. a written judgment *or* a judgment is written—Qal pass. ptc. ms כָּתַב to write; attributive or predicative
7. The word was written in the letters—Qal pass. ptc. ms כָּתַב to write; predicative
8. according to what is written in the law—Qal pass. ptc. ms כָּתַב to write; substantive
9. The woman who was calling with a great voice—Qal act. ptc. fs קָרָא to call; attributive
10. The people who went out were circumcised—Qal act. ptc. mp of יָצָא to go out; attributive; Qal pass. ptc. mp מוּל to circumcise; predicative

Lesson 9

In This Lesson

1. The Independent Personal Pronouns
   third person marked by ה
   second person marked by ת
   first person marked by ־י and ־נוּ
2. The Suffixed Pronouns
   Types A, B and C (see tip 1, below)
   second person marked by כ/ך
3. The Marker of Definite Direct Object: אֵת or ־אֶת
4. The Object Pronouns (see tip 2, below)
5. הִנֵּה: independent and suffixed forms

Terms to Know

definite, indefinite (VI)
gemination (V)
penultimate stress (II)
subject, direct object, indirect object
verbless clause (VII)

Tips

1. Do not try to memorize the "Types" (A, B, C) of pronominal suffixes; after all, the meanings of the suffixes do not change from one type to the next. Concentrate more on the types' similarities than on their differences (chart, p. 97), and let continuing practice be your tutor.

2. Notice the differences between the suffixed pronoun אֵת "with" (IX.2.a, p. 95) and the suffixed forms of the "marker of the definite direct object" (IX.4.a, p. 99). Here is a way to distinguish between these similar forms: if the ת is doubled with a strong *dāgēš* (*'itt-*), the form is the preposition "with"—*with dāgēš* = "with"!

3. Observe that the singular and common plural suffixed forms of כְּ and מִן include an additional archaic element *-mV-* or *-mVn-* (V stands here for any vowel). See also that the 3ms and 1cp forms of suffixed מִן are identical to one another (explained in note on p. 96).

ANSWER KEY

9.a.

1. to them (mp)
2. in it/her
   A *mappîq* in suffixed ה shows it to be a consonant, not a *mater* (II.3.b.iv, p. 8) This will often suggest a Type A 3fs pronominal suffix (chart, p. 97).
3. from me
4. with you (mp)
   The *ʾitt-* element suggests the preposition "with," not an object pronoun. See tip 2, above.
5. with me
6. like it/him
7. with me
   The ד is perhaps a surprise but is in fact predictable in this form (note to chart, p. 95).
8. in them (mp)
   A variant of בָּהֶם (IX.2.a, note 1, p. 95).
9. from them (fp)
10. with them (mp)
11. under (or, in place of) me
12. to you (mp)
13. before you (ms)
    The preposition is לִפְנֵי (VI Vocabulary, p. 60).
14. upon/against you (fs)
15. before me

9.b.

1. בִּי
2. מִמֶּנּוּ
   The form appears identical to "from us" (IX.2.b. note, p. 96).
3. מִמֶּנּוּ
4. אֵלַי

5. עָלַ֫יִךְ
6. מִכֶּם
7. מִכֶּן
8. כָּמ֫וֹהָ
   The *-mô-* element added to the preposition כְּ is regular with the singular suffixed pronouns (IX.2.b, p. 96).
9. עָלַי
10. אֵלֶ֫יךָ or לְךָ
11. אֵלַ֫יִךְ or לָךְ
12. אֵלֶ֫יהָ or לָהּ
13. כָּהֶם
14. אֵלֵ֫ינוּ or לָ֫נוּ
15. כָּמ֫וֹהוּ

9.c.

1. אֲנִי נָבִיא כָּמ֫וֹךָ
   When composing Hebrew, אֲנִי and אָנֹכִי may be considered interchangeable.
2. אָנֹכִי עֹשֶׂה חָדָשׁ
   With substantive use of adjective (VII.3.c, p. 72).
3. אָנֹכִי כֹּרֵת בְּרִית
4. כְּאֵשׁ אֹכֶ֫לֶת
5. כָּבֵד הַדָּבָר מִמְּךָ
   For this comparative use of the preposition מִן, see VII.5.a, p. 73.
6. מַלְאָךְ שָׁלוּחַ אֲלֵיהֶם
   With attributive use of the Qal passive participle (VIII.5.c.i, p. 85).
7. יָד שְׁלוּחָה עָלַי (or אֵלַי)
8. צַדִּיק אַתָּה מִמֶּ֫נִּי
9. כָּמ֫וֹךָ כָּהֶם
   For this idiom, review כְּ in VI Vocabulary, p. 60.
10. הִנְּךָ חָכָם מִן־דָּנִאֵל

9.d.

1. God is with us.
   This is a verbless clause (VI.8, p. 59), not a relative construction (*"God *who* is with us"). In a later chapter you will learn how to construct a relative clause.
2. He is with me.
3. You are handsome.
4. You are beautiful.
5. The ones going up with me
6. The ones guarding me (or, my guardians)
7. The ones eating with him
8. A different spirit is with him.
9. They are with us.
10. And Abraham walked with them.
11. See, the fire and the wood.
12. Look, Rebecca is before you.

9.e. Gen 41:17–20

v 17: וַיְדַבֵּר "(subject) spoke"—בַּחֲלֹמִי "in my dream"—שְׂפַת הַיְאֹר "the bank of the river (i.e., the Nile)": the "Sqnmlwy" letter י in original *הַיְּאֹר loses the expected strong *dāgēš* (VI.1.a, p. 54; VI.7, p. 59).

v 18: בְּרִיאוֹת בָּשָׂר "sturdy of flesh"—וִיפֹת תֹּאַר "and beautiful of form"—וַתִּרְעֶינָה "and they were feeding."

v 19: וְרָעוֹת תֹּאַר מְאֹד "and very ugly of form"—וְרַקּוֹת בָּשָׂר "and thin of flesh"—לֹא־רָאִיתִי "I have never seen"—בְּכָל־אֶרֶץ מִצְרָיִם "in all the land of Egypt."

v 20: וַתֹּאכַלְנָה "and (subject) ate."

REVIEW THE CONCEPTS

1. True or false: The independent pronoun is used for the subject, and the suffixed pronoun may be used for the indirect or direct object.
2. Circle one: In the sentence "I am sending you my servant," "my servant" is the (direct/indirect) object, and "you" is the (direct/indirect) object.

3. Identify the direct and indirect objects: אָנֹכִי שֹׁלֵחַ אֹתָהּ לָהּ

4. Practice the independent suffixed pronouns with photographs of family and friends. Using familiar adjectives and participles, "talk" to and about the women and men in the photos, as in the following examples:

   "He is great" הוּא גָּדוֹל

   "They are great" הֵ֫נָּה גְּדוֹלוֹת

   "I love you (pl)" אֲנִי אֹהֶ֫בֶת אֶתְכֶם

   "We are coming to you" אֲנַ֫חְנוּ הֹלְכִים אֵלֶ֫יךָ

   Doing this "picture album" exercise even five minutes per day will do much for your recognition of pronouns, prepositions, and the Qal participial forms. Try it!

Answers

1. true
2. direct; indirect
3. direct object is אֹתָהּ "her/it" (IX.4, p. 99); indirect object is ָהּ- "her/it" (suffixed to preposition -לְ "to"; IX.2.a, p. 94)
4. Work with a friend to check one another's skills.

Lesson 10

In This Lesson

1. The Demonstratives
   "this/that"—ms זֶה, fs זֹאת
   "these/those"—cp אֵלֶּה
   Pronouns as Demonstratives
   "this/that"—ms הוּא, fs הִיא
   "these/those"—mp הֵם, fp הֵנָּה
   Uses of the Demonstrative: adjective, pronoun, reciprocal/contrast
2. Relative Clauses
   most commonly begin with אֲשֶׁר
   various translations depending on the context (e.g., "which," "when," "whom")
3. The Particle of Existence יֵשׁ
   "there is/there are"
4. The Particle of Negation אֵין
   "there is not/there are not"
5. Differences between Negation Words אֵין and לֹא
   verbless clauses: אֵין
   verbal clauses and single words: לֹא
6. Interrogative Clauses
   interrogative particle ה: at beginning of sentence, introduces question
   "who?" מִי
   "what?" מה
   "how?" אֵיכָה/אֵיךְ
   "where?" אַיֵּה/אֵי
7. Exclamations and Emphatic Questions
   beginning with איך or מה
8. אֲשֶׁר as a Conjunction

Terms to Know

asyndetic
demonstrative
interrogative
reciprocity
resumptive

TIPS

1. A demonstrative may come before or after the noun it modifies, depending on how it is used.

(a) used as pronoun: usually before noun (זֶה הָאִישׁ "this is the man")

(b) used as adjective: after noun (הָאִישׁ הַזֶּה "this man")

Note that these correspond to the positions for attributive and predicative adjectives learned in lesson VII.

2. Remember that various prepositions may be added to מֶה/מָה to form specific interrogatives. Instead of memorizing additional vocabulary words, these can be figured out by combining the meaning of the particular preposition used and מֶה/מָה ("what?"): i.e., לְ ("for") + מָה ("what") = לָמָּה ("for what?" = "why?"). See X.d.iv, p. 110, for other examples.

3. The meanings of some interrogatives and pronouns sound a bit mixed up to English speakers: מִי is "who?"; הוּא is "he"; הִיא is "she"!

4. The letter ה at the beginning of a sentence may indicate a question (think ה = huh?). Do not confuse this with the ה that indicates a definite article. To distinguish these, remember that it is an interrogative ה if it:

(a) takes a composite *šĕwāʾ* (but remember it can also be הַ or הֶ).

(b) does not double the following consonant.

(c) is indicated by the context of the sentence.

ANSWER KEY

10.a.

1. הַגּוֹי הַגָּדוֹל הַזֶּה
   When the demonstrative is used with an adjective, it stands in the final position (X.1.b.i, p. 105). As an attributive, it shares the same characteristics for attributive adjectives (see VII.3.a, p. 72).

2. מִי חָכָם

3. הֲזֶה הָאִישׁ

4. מִי הָאִשָּׁה

5. אַיֵּה הָאֲנָשִׁים

6. הֶעָרִים הָאֵלֶּה

7. הָאֹתוֹת הַגְּדֹלוֹת הָאֵלֶּה

8. אֵלֶּה הָרְשָׁעִים

9. אֵין לָנוּ לֶחֶם

10. אַיֶּכָּה
    See X.6.f, p. 111.

11. מִי לַיהוָה
12. אֵין מֶ֫לֶךְ וְאֵין שַׂר
13. מִי כָמֹ֫וךָ
14. אִישׁ שֹׁכֵב עִם אִשָּׁה
15. מָה אַתֶּם עֹשִׂים
16. אֵין הַנַּ֫עַר אִתָּנוּ
17. הֲזֹאת הָעִיר הַגְּדוֹלָה
18. אִישׁ מֹשֵׁל בְּיִשְׂרָאֵל
    Note that the verb מָשַׁל takes an object marked by the preposition בְּ; see Vocabulary X, p. 113.
19. יֵשׁ יְהוָה בַּמָּקוֹם הַזֶּה
20. הֲיֵשׁ־לָכֶם אָח

10.b.

1. Peace, peace, but there is no peace.
2. There is nothing good for humanity under the sun.
3. the land on which you are lying
   For the resumptive element at the end of the clause, see X.2.a, p. 106.
4. There is a God judging on the earth *or* There is a God who judges on the earth.
5. How many are my iniquities and sins?
6. What are these stones to you?
7. Who knows what is good for humanity in life?
8. both you and this people who are with you
   In Exod 18:18, the suffix refers to Moses and is thus 2ms, not 2fs. This is an example of the 2ms form in pause. See Excursus B, 5.a, p. 67, and IX.2. note ii, p. 95.
9. because the matter is too heavy for you
   For the comparative use of מִן, see VII.5.a, p. 73.
10. Do you not see what they are doing?
    Lit. "Is there not (for) you a seeing (of) what they are doing?" The הַ is an interrogative הַ before the guttural א, not the definite article. Compare X.6.b.ii, p. 109, with VI.1.b.i, p. 54.

11. he and the men who are with him
12. What is this evil thing that you are doing?
13. What is this thing that you are doing for the people?
14. Why are you sitting by yourself?
15. This is not the way, and this is not the city.
16. There is no one greater in this house than I.
17. Who is this coming up from the wilderness?
18. I am sending a messenger before you.
19. And Abraham was still standing before YHWH.
    The 3ms suffix on עוֹדֶנּוּ is resumptive and does not need to be translated. For the form, see IX.2.b.note, p. 96.
20. I am YHWH, and there is no one else:
    one who fashions light and creates darkness,
    who makes peace and creates evil.

10.c. Deut 29:12–14

v 12: לְמַ֫עַן הָקִים "so that he (i.e., YHWH) may establish"—יִהְיֶה "will be"—דִּבֶּר "he spoke"—נִשְׁבַּע "he swore"—לַאֲבֹתֶיךָ "to your forebears"

v 14: For יֶשְׁנוֹ, see X.3.b, p. 107—אֱלֹהֵינוּ "our God."

Review the Concepts

Write the following phrases in Hebrew:

1. This is the throne.
2. This throne is for the king.

Match the following to its correct Hebrew translation.

3. this law

   a. הַתּוֹרָה הַזֶּה   b. זֹאת הַתּוֹרָה   c. הַתּוֹרָה הַזֹּאת

4. Where is the sun?

   a. אֵי הַשֶּׁמֶשׁ   b. אֵיךְ הַשֶּׁמֶשׁ   c. אַיֵּה שֶׁמֶשׁ

5. Why does he weep?

   a. לָמָה בֹּכֶה   b. עַד־מָה בֹּכֶה   c. עַל־מָה בֹּכֶה

6. There are no signs.

   a. אֵין אוֹתִים　　b. יֵשׁ אוֹתִים　　c. אֵין אוֹתוֹת

7. after those times

   a. אַחֲרֵי הָעִתִּים הָאֵ֫לֶּה　　b. אַחֲרֵי הָעִתִּים הָהֵם

   c. כַּאֲשֶׁר הָעִתִּים הָהֵם

8. because of peace

   a. עֵ֫קֶב אֲשֶׁר שָׁלוֹם　　b. כַּאֲשֶׁר שָׁלוֹם　　c. יַ֫עַן אֲשֶׁר שָׁלוֹם

9. the lad who falls

   a. הַנַּ֫עַר אֲשֶׁר מֹשֵׁךְ　　b. הַנַּ֫עַר אֲשֶׁר נֹפֵל　　c. הַנַּ֫עַר אֲשֶׁר נָפַל

10. Does he have a servant?

   a. אֵין לוֹ אֶ֫בֶן　　b. יֵשׁ לוֹ עֶ֫בֶד　　c. הֲיֵשׁ לוֹ עֶ֫בֶד

Answers

1. זֶה הַכִּסֵּא
2. הַכִּסֵּא הַזֶּה לַמֶּ֫לֶךְ
3. c
4. a
5. a, c
6. c
7. a, b
   The plural form of עֵת is עִתִּים.
8. a, c
9. b
10. c

Lesson 11

In This Lesson

1. The Construct Chain
2. Construct Noun Forms
3. Participles and Adjectives in Construct Chains
4. Translation of the Construct Chain
5. The Forms and Uses of כֹּל
6. The Superlative

Terms to Know

absolute state
construct chain
construct state
definite (VI)
indefinite (VI)

Tips

1. Construct Noun Forms:
   (a) ms nouns: minor vowel changes or no change
   (b) mp and dual nouns: ִים -, ַ֫יִם - becomes ֵי -; minor vowel changes or no change
   (c) fs nouns: ָה - becomes ַת -, minor vowel changes or no change
   (d) fp nouns: וֹת is retained; minor vowel changes or no change

2. Remember: a noun is definite if it is a proper name, has a definite article, or has a suffixed pronoun (IX.3.a, p. 98).

3. If the absolute noun is indefinite, the construct chain is indefinite. If the absolute noun is definite, the construct chain is definite.

4. Adjectives and demonstratives do not normally interrupt the construct chain; they will stand after the absolute noun.

5. The construct chain is not used to show possession between an indefinite noun and a definite noun; לְ is used in such cases.

6. When functioning as substantives, adjectives and participles may appear in construct chains.

7. Note the list of unpredictable construct forms (p. 121).

ANSWER KEY

11.a.

1. מְקוֹם
   In an open syllable *ā* or *ē* reduces to *šĕwāʾ* (XI.2.d, p. 118).

2. יַם
   The vowel *ā* in a final closed syllable becomes *a* (XI.2.b, p. 118).

3. שְׂדֵה
   Final הֶ - becomes הֵ - (XI.2.f, p. 119).

4. בָּתֵּי
   The plural ending ִים - changes to ֵי - (XI.2.c, p. 118).

5. אַנְשֵׁי
   If vowel reduction results in two vocal *šĕwāʾ*s, the Rule of *Šĕwāʾ* applies (XI.2.d, note ii, p. 119).

6. אַרְצוֹת

7. עַמֵּי

8. עַבְדֵי
   Segolate plurals retain their base vowel (XI.2.i, p. 120).

9. אֲבִי
   This is an unpredictable construct form (see list, p. 121).

10. אֲחִי
    This is an unpredictable construct form (see list, p. 121).

11. תּוֹךְ
    Original *aw contracts to *ô* (XI.2.g, p. 119).

12. שְׁמוֹת

13. נַפְשׁוֹת

14. פְּנֵי
    The plural ending ִים - changes to ֵי -; in an open syllable *ā* or *ē* reduces to *šĕwāʾ* (XI.2.c–d, p. 118).

15. רָאשֵׁי

16. כְּלֵי
    The plural ending ִים - changes to ֵי -; in an open syllable *ā* or *ē* reduces to *šĕwāʾ* (XI.2.c–d, p. 118).

17. שָׂרֵי
    When *ā* or *ē* is the result of compensatory lengthening, the long vowel is not reduced (XI.2.d, note i, pp. 118–19).

18. עֲדַת
Femimine ־ָה - becomes ־ַת - (XI.2.e, p. 119).

19. יֵין
Original *ay contracts to *ê* (XI.2.h, p. 120). The unchanged form יַ֫יִן is also attested in construct (BDB יַ֫יִן, p. 406).

20. מַעֲשֵׂה

21. עֲפַר
The vowel *ā* in a final closed syllable becomes *a;* in an open syllable *ā* or *ē* reduces to *šĕwāʾ* (XI.2.b, d, p. 118).

22. סִפְרֵי
Segolate plurals retain their base vowel (XI.2.i, p. 120).

23. רַגְלֵי
The dual ending ־ַ֫יִם - becomes ־ֵי - (XI.2.c, p. 118).

24. בְּנוֹת

11.b.

1. אַחִים
This is an unpredictable construct form (see list, p. 121).

2. דִּבְרֵי
If vowel reduction results in two vocal *šĕwāʾ*s, the Rule of *Šĕwāʾ* applies (XI.2.d, note ii, p. 119).

3. אֹהָלִים
One expects the plural absolute אֳהָלִים (V.2.c, p. 42; XI.2.i.i, p. 120), but the attested absolute form is that given here, retaining the *ḥṓlem.*

4. דְּרָכִים

5. כְּנָפַ֫יִם
The absolute plural form is unattested.

6. דָּמִים
The plural ending ־ִים - changes to ־ֵי -; in an open syllable *ā* or *ē* reduces to *šĕwāʾ* (XI.2.c–d, p. 118).

7. מְלָאכָה
See Vocabulary, p. 125.

8. אִשָּׁה
This is an unpredictable construct form (see list, p. 121).

9. נָשִׁים

10. מִלְחָמָה
This is an unpredictable construct form (see list, p. 121).

11. יָמִים (days)

12. יַמִּים (seas)

13. מַ֫יִם (water)

14. עֵינַ֫יִם
The absolute plural form is unattested.

15. כֵּלִים
See V Vocabulary, p. 44.

16. אַ֫יִל

17. עָרִים
This is an unpredictable construct form (see list, p. 121).

18. אָח
This is an unpredictable construct form (see list, p. 121).

19. חוֹמָה

20. שָׁנִים

21. שָׁמַ֫יִם

22. פֶּה
This is an unpredictable construct form (see list, p. 121).

23. זָקֵן
Nouns of the *qāṭēl* pattern become *qĕṭal* in construct (XI.2.j, p. 121).

24. מָ֫וֶת
Original **aw* contracts to *ô* (XI.2.g, p. 119).

11.c.

1. And these are the names of the Israelites (lit., "sons of Israel")
The construct chain is definite because the absolute noun is definite (XI.1.b, p. 116).

2. I am the God of Abraham.

3. After the death of Moses, the servant of YHWH

4. A work of human hands
Note the adjectival use of the construct chain (XI.4, p. 122).

5. Like the appearance of the angel of God

6. And there was no bread in the whole land, for the famine was very severe.

7. And look, the angels of God were going up and down on it.

8. And the appearance of the glory of YHWH was like a consuming fire on the top of the mountain.

9. Why (indeed) are you transgressing the command of YHWH?
Often זֶה is added to make a question emphatic (X.7.b, p. 111).

10. The one who gives rain upon the surface of (the) earth and who sends water upon the surface of (the) open country
This example is poetic Hebrew from Job 5:10; poetic Hebrew often lacks an expected definite article (this will be explained in Excursus E).

11. Do you not see what they are doing in the cities of Judah and in the streets of Jerusalem?

12. And every person of Judah and all the inhabitants of Jerusalem were with him and the priests and the prophets and all of the people, both young and old.
For the translation of כל here, see XI.5.b.ii–iii, p. 123. For the translation of עַד ... מִן, see BDB מִן 5.b, pp. 581–82.

11.d. 2 Chr 5:1–10

v 1: וַתִּשְׁלַם "when (subject) was completed"—עָשָׂה "(subject) accomplished"—וַיָּבֵא "(subject) brought"—אָבִיו "his father"—נָתַן "he put."

v 2: יַקְהֵיל "(subject) assembled"—לְהַעֲלוֹת "to bring up"—הִיא For the use of הִיא here, see IX.1.b.iv, p. 94.

v 3: וַיִּקָּהֲלוּ "(subject) assembled themselves."

v 4: וַיָּבֹאוּ "(subject) came"—וַיִּשְׂאוּ "and (subject) carried."

v 5: וַיַּעֲלוּ "and (subject) brought (object) up"—הֶעֱלוּ "they brought (object) up."

v 6: עֲדַת is the construct of עֵדָה; for the location of this noun in BDB, review Excursus A, p. 51—הַנּוֹעָדִים "who had gathered themselves"—מְזַבְּחִים "were sacrificing"—לֹא־יִסָּפְרוּ "could not be counted"—וְלֹא יִמָּנוּ "and could not be numbered"—מֵרֹב (= מִן + רֹב) "because of (their) abundance."

v 7: וַיָּבִיאוּ "and (subject) brought (object) in"—מְקוֹמוֹ "its place."

v 8: וַיִּהְיוּ "and (subject) were"—וַיְכַסּוּ "and (subject) covered"—בַּדָּיו "its poles"—מִלְמָעְלָה "from above."

v 9: וַיַּאֲרִיכוּ "and (subject) extended"—וַיֵּרָאוּ "and (subject) were visible"—וְלֹא יֵרָאוּ "but they were not visible"—הַחוּצָה "from outside"—וַיְהִי "and it has been."

v 10: רַק "only"—שְׁנֵי "the two"—נָתַן "(subject) gave"—כָּרַת "(subject) had made (i.e., the covenant)"—בְּצֵאתָם "when they went out."

REVIEW THE CONCEPTS

Translate

1. בֵּן לְדָוִד
2. עֶבֶד דָּוִד
3. עָרֵי יִשְׂרָאֵל
4. עֵינֵי הַמֶּלֶךְ
5. אֶל־אֶרֶץ זָבַת חָלָב וּדְבָשׁ

Parse זָבַת

Answers

1. a son of David
2. the servant of David
3. the cities of Israel
4. the eyes of the king
5. to a land flowing with milk and honey
   Qal act. ptc. fs (construct) זוּב to flow. The absolute form of the fs participle, זָבָה, becomes זָבַת in construct (XI.2.e, p. 119). For translation, see XI.4, p. 122.

Lesson 12

In This Lesson

1. Nouns with Pronominal Suffixes
2. Forms of the Nouns before Suffixes
   polysyllabic nouns
   geminate nouns
   segolate nouns
   nouns with diphthongs
   nouns with III-*Wāw/Yōḏ* roots
   the nouns בֵּן (son) and שֵׁם (name)
   the nouns אִשָּׁה (woman, wife) and בַּת (daughter)

Terms to Know

construct
diphthongs (III)
geminate nouns (V)
segolate nouns (V)

Tips

1. Suffixed pronouns are attached to the construct form of the noun.

2. As in lesson IX, do not focus on memorizing the details of each type. Rather, learn to recognize the suffixed pronouns by their common markers. For the 1cs suffixed pronoun, however, learn to distinguish the Type A form (ִי) used with singular nouns from the Type C form (ַי) used with plural nouns.

3. When plural construct forms take pronominal suffixes, the vowel with the י-*mater* will be that of the Type C suffixes. Review the summary of Pronominal Suffixes on pages 97–98 and note the examples in this lesson.

4. Note: אָבִי (my father) and אֲבִי (father of).

Answer Key

12.a.

1. אַפָּהּ
   אַף is a **qall* geminate noun that was originally **qanl*. See XII.2.b, p. 136; V.1.a, pp. 38–39.

2. אֲנָשָׁיו
3. שָׂדֵהוּ
   For singular nouns that end in ה ֶ-, see XII.2.e, note ii, p. 140.
4. פְּרָיִם
   For nouns like פְּרִי, see XII.2.e, note iii, p. 141.
5. פִּרְיִי
6. מַלְכֵּ֫נוּ
7. אִשְׁתּוֹ
   For the presuffix form of this noun, see XII.2.g, p. 142.
8. שְׁמִי
   The stem vowel (*ṣērê*) reduces before the suffix; see XII.2.f, p. 141.
9. עֻזָּהּ\כֹּחָהּ
10. נָשָׁיו
11. עָרֶ֫יךָ
    This is an unpredictable construct form (see list, p. 121).
12. עַמִּי
13. אָבִ֫ינוּ
14. יָדָיו
15. פִּיו/פִּ֫יהוּ
16. מַעֲשֵׂ֫ינוּ
17. רוּחֲכֶם
18. עָנָן כָּבֵד
19. בֵּתִי
    For the presuffix form of this noun, see XII.2.g, p. 142.
20. מַטְּךָ
21. אָחִ֫יךָ
22. אַחֶ֫יךָ
23. זַרְעֲךָ
24. בְּגָדֶ֫יהָ

12.b.

1. the breath of our nostrils

2. your strong ark
   The construct chain is definite if the absolute noun is definite (XI.1.b, p. 116). Note the adjectival use of the construct chain (XI.4, p. 122).
3. a strong tower
4. the ivory houses
   For this plural form, review Irregular Plurals, p. 43.
5. our father is old
6. your splendid garments
7. the holy garments
8. all the days of my life
9. like the ivory tower
10. a great ivory throne
11. all the men of his house
12. your cloud is standing upon them
13. God of our fathers/the gods of our fathers
14. a breath of life was in his nostrils
15. their mothers who bore them
    For the form אִמּוֹת, see V.1.b, note i, p. 39.

12.c.

1. Who knows the strength (fierceness) of your anger?
2. For your faithfulness is better than life.
   For the comparative use of מִן, see VII.5.a, p. 73.
3. This is the camp of God.
4. And your faithfulness is like a morning cloud.
5. There is no one like you among the gods, O Lord, and there is nothing like your works.
   For the form כָּמ֫וֹךָ, review IX.2.b, p. 96. For the translation of אֲדֹנָי, see BDB אָדוֹן 3.b, p. 11.
6. Our holy and beautiful house
7. There is no one who pitches my tent any longer.
8. YHWH's name is a strong tower.

9. An eternal statute for him and for his seed after him

10. And my spirit is standing (abiding) in your midst.
For the noun in the phrase בְּתוֹכְכֶם, review construct noun forms (XI.2.g, p. 119).

11. I am YHWH, the one who makes everything, who stretches the heavens by myself.
For לְבַדִּי, see X Vocabulary, p. 112.

12. I am about to put my words in your mouth as fire.
For this use of the participle, review VIII.4.a.iii, p. 82.

13. And they are not doing according to their statutes and according to their judgments, and according to the law, and according to the commandment.

14. The ark of the covenant, the Lord of all the earth, is passing before you *or* The ark of the covenant of the Lord of all the earth is passing before you.
Many versions (e.g., KJV, NRSV, NIV, NJPS) translate this verse as: "The ark of the covenant of the Lord of all the earth is passing before you." This translation apparently assumes that the article with בְּרִית is a violation of the rule for construct chains, which states that nouns in construct cannot take the article (XI.1, p. 116; see also Excursus D.2, p. 131, for a similar example from Jer 25:26).
Alternatively, the two construct chains may be interpreted as appositional and translated as (cf. Josh 3:13): "The ark of the covenant, the Lord of all the earth, is passing before you."

15. All the servants of Pharaoh, the elders of his house, and all the elders of the land of Egypt

12.d. Ps 121

v 1: אֶשָּׂא "I will lift up"—מֵאַ֫יִן interrogative adverb (X.6.f, p. 111)—יָבֹא "will come."

v 2: מֵעִם combination of מִן + עִם (VI.5.b.ii, p. 57).

v 3: אַל־יִתֵּן לַמּוֹט "may he not permit (object) to stumble"—רַגְלֶ֫ךָ segolate noun רֶ֫גֶל (*qatl*) + suffix; we would expect the form רַגְלְךָ (XII.2.c, pp. 137–38), but here the form is in pause (Excursus B.5, pp. 67–68)—אַל־יָנוּם "may (subject) not slumber"—שֹׁמְרֶ֫ךָ participle of שֹׁמֵר + suffix; the *ṣērê* reduces according to the rules in III.2.a, pp. 19–20, and here the form is in pause; this same form appears in v 5 below.

v 4: לֹא־יָנוּם וְלֹא יִישָׁן "he will not slumber and he will not sleep."

v 5: צִלְּךָ geminate noun צֵל (*qill) + suffix (XII.2.b, p. 136)—יְמִינֶךָ noun יָמִין + suffix, pausal form.

v 6: לֹא־יַכֶּכָּה "will not smite you."

v 7: יִשְׁמָרְךָ "will keep you"—יִשְׁמֹר "he will keep"—נַפְשֶׁךָ segolate noun נֶ֫פֶשׁ (*qatl) + suffix, pausal form.

v 8: יִשְׁמָר־צֵאתְךָ וּבוֹאֶךָ "will guard your going and coming"—מֵעַתָּה combination of מִן + עַתָּה (VI.5.b.ii, pp. 57–58).

REVIEW THE CONCEPTS

Matching

1. דְּבָרֵ֫נוּ	a. her word
2. דְּבָרַי	b. his words
3. דְּבָרָיו	c. our word
4. דְּבָרָן	d. your (fp) words
5. דְּבָרָהּ	e. my word
6. דִּבְרֵיכֶן	f. their (mp) word
7. דְּבָרֶ֫יהָ	g. their (fp) word
8. דְּבָרָם	h. her words
9. דְּבָרֶ֫יךָ	i. your (ms) words
10. דְּבָרִי	j. my words

Answers

1. c	6. d
2. j	7. h
3. b	8. f
4. g	9. i
5. a	10. e

Lesson 13

In This Lesson

1. The Afformatives of the Perfect
2. The Qal Perfect (see the chart on p. 146)
   dynamic, typically שָׁמַר
   stative, typically כָּבֵד or קָטֹן
3. Uses of the Perfect
   aspect, not tense
   translation of the perfect
4. Syntax of the Verbal Clause
   normal word order
   disrupted word order
   agreement of subject
5. Negation of the Perfect
   לֹא followed by a perfect verb
6. The Directive ָה -
7. Construct Chains (continued)

Terms to Know

afformative
aspect (perfect or imperfect)
construct chain (XI)
disjunctive ו
dynamic verbs
negation (X)
perfect inflection
stative verbs

Tips

1. In earlier chapters, we have used the word *suffix* for elements added to a word. The endings of the perfect verbal inflection are better called "afformatives," because they are added to the root (not to words). In fact, in a later chapter we will add true suffixes to the perfect verb!

2. The word *perfect* can refer to two distinguishable but related concepts: the form of the verb and its function. See the discussion on the perfect *aspect* (function) of the perfect verbal *inflection* (form): XIII.3, pp. 147–49.

3. The Hebrew perfect verb is not marked for *tense,* or time (XIII.3, pp. 147–49). The perfect verb can refer to events past, present, or future.

4. The directive ָה- stands out from other, similar-looking suffixes in that it is not accented.

Answer Key

13.a.

1. אָכַ֫לְתִּי
2. כָּתַ֫בְנוּ
3. נָתַ֫תִּי
   The third radical may assimilate to the afformative (XIII.2, note iii, p. 147).
4. כָּרַ֫תְנוּ
5. לָקַ֫חְתִּי
   Observe that III-Guttural roots are regular in the Qal perfect; this and other "weak" forms will be learned in the next lesson.
6. נָתַנּוּ
   See comment on no. 3 above.
7. הָלַ֫כְתִּי
8. נָתְנוּ
9. מָשַׁח
10. חָזַק
11. לָקְחוּ
12. זָקַ֫נְתִּי
    No assimilation of the נ: the final נ of the verbal root assimilates to a suffixed תּ- only in the root נתן (XIII.2, note iii, p. 147).
13. לָקְחָה
14. עָזְבוּ
15. חָזְקָה
16. יָרְאָה
17. זָכַ֫רְנוּ
18. שָׁמַרְתְּ
19. כָּרַ֫תְּ
    Again, see XIII.2, note iii, p. 147.

20. זְכַרְתֶּם
21. זָכְרָה
22. הָלַכְתְּ
23. כָּבְדָה
24. לְקַחְתֶּם

13.b.

1. See, fire came down from heaven.
2. Because you said, "We have made a covenant with death."
   Direct and indirect discourse must often be discerned on the basis of context alone, in this case by the verb אֲמַרְתֶּם.
3. You love evil more than good.
   For this comparative use of מִן, see VII.5.a, p. 73.
4. It is the bread that YHWH gave to you.
5. Is this your youngest brother (of) whom you spoke to me?
   For this superlative sense of the adjective ("youngest"), see XI.6, p. 124.
6. Now I have given to you a wise heart.
7. He did not eat food all day and all night.
8. He heard that they had anointed him as king in place of his father.
   The disrupted word order emphasizes the direct object (XIII.4.b.iii, p. 151).
9. God reigns over nations; God sits on his holy throne.
   With adjectival use of construct chain (XI.4, p. 122).
10. I am old; I do not know the day of my death.
    Not "I was old" (XIII.3.c, p. 148).

13.c. Ps 136

Study tip: Many English translations supply the English verb "endure" for the phrase לְעוֹלָם חַסְדּוֹ. One sees, however, that this is a verbless clause: "His devotion (is) forever" (VI.8, p. 59).

v 1: הוֹדוּ "give thanks!"—טוֹב "is good" (here טוֹב is the stative Qal perf. 3ms of the root טוֹב "to be good, pleasing").

v 3: לַאֲדֹנֵי is plural in form but has a singular meaning; see III.1.g, p. 19; IV Vocabulary, p. 35.

v 4: נִפְלָאוֹת "wonders"—The verse begins with לְ + participle and presumes (from vv 1–3) the imperative הוֹדוּ. Thus, "(Give praise) to the one who. . ." (the same comment applies to 5–7, 10, 13, 16, 17). For translation of the participles, review VIII.4.c, p. 83.

v 8: The definite direct object (marked by אֶת) is the object of the participle beginning v 7 (so also v 9). For the translation of לְמֶמְשֶׁלֶת here and of לְמֶמְשְׁלוֹת in v 9, see BDB מֶמְשָׁלָה 2, p. 606.

v 10: לְמַכֵּה "to the one who smites" (so also v 17).

v 11: וַיּוֹצֵא "and led."

v 14: וְהֶעֱבִיר "and he caused (object) to pass through."

v 15: וְנִעֵר "and he threw off."

v 16: לְמוֹלִיךְ "to the one who leads (object)."

v 19: לְסִיחוֹן the preposition לְ here and in v 20 marks the person against whom an action is directed; see BDB לְ 3.b, pp. 511–12.

v 23: שֶׁבְּשִׁפְלֵנוּ = שֶׁ + בְּ + שֵׁפֶל + 1cp suffix.

v 24: וַיִּפְרְקֵנוּ "and he tore us away."

Review the Concepts

Remembering that the perfect aspect has many uses (XIII.3, pp. 147–49), translate the following.

1. זָקַנְתִּי מִן־הַדָּבָר הַזֶּה
2. יָדַעְנוּ לִבְּךָ
3. הַשָּׂדֶה נָתַתִּי לָךְ
4. בַּיּוֹם הַזֶּה זָכְרוּ עַמִּי אֹתִי

Answers

1. I *am* too *old* for this matter (not "I *was*. . ."; stative verb).
2. *We know* your mind (not "We *knew*. . ."; verb of perception).
3. The field *I* (hereby) *give* to you (not "I *gave*. . ."; instantaneous occurrence).
4. In that day, my people *will remember* me (not "*remembered*. . ."; certainty of occurrence; for the word order, see XIII.4, pp. 149–50).

Lesson 14

In This Lesson

1. The Qal Perfect of Guttural Verbs
   gutturals prefer *a*-class vowels and composite *šĕwāʾ* (lesson II)
2. The Qal Perfect of III-*ʾĀlep̄* Verbs
   quiescent א (lesson II)
3. The Qal Perfect of III-*Hē* Verbs
   loss of the final weak radical (lesson IV)
4. The Qal Perfect of II-*Wāw/Yōḏ* Verbs
   loss of the middle-weak radical (lesson IV)
5. Stative Verbs
6. Uses of הָיָה
7. Impersonal Constructions

Terms to Know

aspect (XIII)
dynamic verbs (XIII)
impersonal construction
perfect inflection (XIII)
stative verbs (XIII)
verbless clause (VI)

Tips

1. The Qal perfect 3ms form of II-*Wāw/Yōḏ* verbs is identical to the Qal active participle ms (e.g., בָּא, קָם). If the form is before the subject, it is probably the perfect; if it is after the subject, it is probably the participle (XIV.4.a, note ii, p. 163).

2. The Qal perfect 3fs form of II-*Wāw/Yōḏ* verbs looks very similar to the Qal active participle fs, but the perfect form has the accent on the first syllable, while the participle does not; e.g., קָ֫מָה, קָמָה (XIV.4.a, note iii, p. 163).

3. The Qal perfect 3cp of II-*Wāw/Yōḏ* verbs looks very similar to the Qal perfect 3cp of III-*Hē* verbs, but the former has an accent on the first syllable, while the latter does not; e.g., שָׁ֫בוּ from שׁוּב, but שָׁבוּ from שָׁבָה (XIV.4.a, note iv, p. 163).

4. The Perfect of הָיָה may be:
   (a) used to state a past fact;

(b) used to indicate existence or absence in the past;
(c) used to indicate possession in a past time; or
(d) translated as "to come," "to come to pass," "to become," or "to happen."

Answer Key

14.a.

1. Qal perf. 1cs מָלֵא to fill
In the Qal perfect of III-*ʾÁlep̄* roots the א quiesces and the second syllable takes a long vowel (XIV.2, p. 160-1).

2. Qal perf. 2ms עָשָׂה to make, do
In the Qal perfect of III-*Hē* roots the first- and second-person forms have י after the second radical (XIV.3.a, note iii, p. 161).

3. Qal perf. 1cs בּוֹשׁ to be ashamed
In the Qal perfect of II-*Wāw/Yōḏ* roots the middle radical disappears (XIV.4.a, p. 162). בּוֹשׁ is a stative verb (XIV.4.b, p. 164).

4. Qal perf. 1cs הָיָה to be, become
The verb הָיָה is both I-Guttural and III-*Hē* (XIV.3.b, pp. 161–62).

5. Qal perf. 3fs מוּת to die

6. Qal act. ptc. fs בּוֹא to come, enter
The Qal perfect 3fs form of II-*Wāw/Yōḏ* roots has an accent on the first syllable; the Qal active participle does not; see no. 7 below (XIV.4.a, note iii, p. 163).

7. Qal perf. 3fs בּוֹא to come, enter

8. Qal perf. 3cp גּוּר to sojourn

9. Qal perf. 3fs הָיָה to be, become

10. Qal perf. 2fs חָטָא to sin

11. Qal perf. 3cp הָיָה to be, become

12. Qal act. ptc. fs חָטָא to sin
For this form, review VIII.3.d, p. 80.

13. Qal perf. 1cs מוּת to die

14. Qal perf. 1cs סוּר to turn aside

15. Qal perf. 1cp מוּת to die

14.b.

1. בָּחֲרוּ
   II-Guttural roots will take a composite *šĕwā'* with the guttural (XIV.1.b, p. 160).
2. שָׂמָה
   The Qal perfect 3ms form of II-*Wāw/Yōḏ* roots has an accent on the first syllable (XIV.4.a, note iii, p. 163).
3. עָשִׂיתִי
4. שָׂמוּ
5. מֵת
6. הֱיִיתֶם
7. מַתָּה
   See XIV.4.b, p. 164.
8. עָלְתָה
9. עֲשִׂיתֶם
10. חָיִיתָ
11. בָּאתָ
12. גָּר
    The Qal perfect 3ms form of II-*Wāw/Yōḏ* verbs is identical to the Qal active participle ms (XIV.4.a, note ii, p. 163).
13. נָשָׂאתָ
14. בֹּשְׁנוּ
15. עֲזַבְתֶּם
    I-Guttural roots will take a composite *šĕwā'* with the guttural (XIV.1.a, p. 160).

14.c.

1. Where are the men who came to you tonight?
   For אַיֵּה, review X.6.f, p. 111.
2. We were very ashamed because we had abandoned (the) land.
3. We do not know what has happened to him.
   For the translation of הָיָה, see XIV.6.d, p. 166.

4. Look, my eye has seen everything, my ear has heard (it).
   For the form and use of הֶן, review IX.5, pp. 99–100. The disrupted word order here may be for emphasis, but in poetic texts order may vary for stylistic reasons (XIII.4.b, note, p. 151).

5. And this is the instruction that Moses set before the Israelites.

6. My lord asked his servants (saying), "Do you have a father or brother?"
   For the translation of הֲיֵשׁ־לְ X, review X.3.c, p. 108.

7. And you yourselves know the life of a sojourner, for you were sojourners in the land of Egypt.
   For the use of the independent pronoun for emphasis, see IX.1.b.ii, p. 93.

8. Has this happened in your days or in the days of your fathers?
   For the form בִּימֵי, review XI.2.c, p. 118; VI.3.a, p. 56.

9. And before him there was no king like him, who turned to YHWH with his whole heart.
   For the translation of הָיָה, see XIV.6.b, pp. 165–66.

10. However, the daughter of Pharoah went up from the city of David to her house that he built for her.

14.d. Eccl 2:4–10

v 4: הִגְדַּלְתִּי "I accomplished (greatly)."

v 5: For the translation of כֹּל here, review XI.5.b.iii, p. 123.

v 6: לְהַשְׁקוֹת "to irrigate."

v 7: הָיָה לִי (both times) "there was to me" (impersonal use)—הַרְבֵּה "abundantly."

v 8: בֶּן־אָדָם often simply means "human being, a member of humanity," indicating membership in a class (see BDB בֵּן 7.a, p. 121); the plural construct here is adjectival (XI.4, p. 122)—The meaning of שִׁדָּה is uncertain (BDB, p. 994). In addition to the possibility of "concubine, harem" followed by many translations (e.g., NIV, NASB, NRSV), the word can also be translated as "chest, coffer"; thus NJPS translates the phrase as "coffers and coffers of them."

v 9: וְהוֹסַפְתִּי "and I increased"—For the use -שֶׁ, see X.2.b, p. 106–7.

REVIEW THE CONCEPTS

Parse the following forms:

1. מְצָאתֶם
2. הָיִית
3. שָׂמָה
4. גָּר
5. בָּשְׁתֶּן
6. סַ֫רְנוּ
7. שָׂ֫מָה
8. קַמְתְּ
9. נָֽשְׂאָה
10. גָּרָה

Answers

1. Qal perf. 2mp מָצָא to find
2. Qal perf. 2fs הָיָה to be
3. Qal act. ptc. fs שִׂים to set
4. Qal act. ptc. ms or Qal perf. 3ms of גּוּר to sojourn
5. Qal perf. 2fp בּוֹשׁ to be ashamed
6. Qal perf. 1cp סוּר to turn aside
7. Qal perf. 3fs שִׂים to set
8. Qal perf. 2fs קוּם to arise
9. Qal perf. 3fs נָשָׂא to lift up
10. Qal act. ptc. fs גּוּר to sojourn

LESSON 15

IN THIS LESSON

1. The Piel Perfect Form: strong verb קִטֵּל; weak roots see chart at XV.1, p. 173
2. The Meaning of Verbs in Piel
   factitive, intensive, denominative, declarative, other
3. The Piel Perfect Form of II-Guttural and II-*Rêš* Verbs
   expect compensatory lengthening or virtual doubling
4. The Piel Perfect Form of III-*ʾĀlep̄* Verbs
5. The Piel Perfect Form of III-*Hē* Verbs
6. The Piel Perfect Form of II-*Wāw/Yōd* Verbs
7. The Form of the Piel Participle: מְקַטֵּל
   see synopsis of participial forms (XV.7, p. 177)

TERMS TO KNOW

declarative
denominative
factitive
intensive

TIPS

1. The Piel perfect has these key characteristics (קִטֵּל):
   (a) *ḥîreq* under the first radical
   (b) doubling of the second radical
2. The Piel participle has these key characteristics (מְקַטֵּל):
   (a) *šĕwāʾ* under the מ prefix
   (b) doubling of the second radical
   (c) *e*-class vowel (sometimes reduced) under second root radical in masculine forms and most feminine forms

ANSWER KEY

15.a.

1. Piel perf. 2mp of בִּקֵּשׁ to seek
2. Piel perf. 2ms of דִּבֵּר to speak

3. Piel perf. 3cp of כָּלָה to finish
4. Qal perf. 3fs of כָּלָה to be complete
5. Piel perf. 2ms of כָּסָה to cover
6. Piel ptc. fs of דָּבַר to speak
7. Piel perf. 3cp of בָּרַךְ to bless
   In some cases, a composite *šĕwāʾ* may appear under a ר instead of a regular vocal *šĕwāʾ*; see GKC, §10.g, p. 53 (on GKC, see Excursus D).
8. Piel perf. 3fs of בָּקַשׁ to seek
   "Sqnmlwy" with loss of strong *dāgēš* in the ק (VI.7, p. 59; XV.1, note ii, p. 173)
9. Qal perf. 1cp of כָּלָה to be complete
10. Piel perf. 2fs of דָּבַר to speak
11. Piel perf. 2mp of הָלַל to praise
12. Piel ptc. ms of כָּלָה to finish
13. Piel ptc. mp of בָּקַשׁ to seek
   "Sqnmlwy" with loss of strong *dāgēš* in the ק (VI.7, p. 59; XV.7, note, p. 177)
14. Piel perf. 1cs of כָּסָה to cover
   The Piel perf. 1cs form occurs both as כִּסִּ֫יתִי and as כִּסֵּ֫יתִי (BDB, p. 491).
15. Piel ptc. ms of בָּרַךְ to bless

15.b.

1. בֵּרַ֫כְתִּי
2. בִּקֵּשׁ
3. מִהֲרוּ
4. מִלֵּ֫אתִי
5. מִהֲרָה
6. שֵׁרְתוּ
7. סִפְּרוּ
8. כִּלָּה
9. צִוִּ֫יתִי
   Also occurs as צִוֵּ֫יתִי (BDB, p. 845).

10. פָּעֲלוּ
11. כִּלִּיתֶם
12. סִפַּרְתֶּם
13. מִהַ֫רְתָּ
14. קִדַּשְׁתֶּם
15. צִוָּה

15.c.

1. We sinned because we spoke against YHWH and against you.
   In Num 21:7 the suffix refers to Moses and is thus 2ms rather than 2fs. This is an example of the 2ms form in pause (see Excursus B.5.a, p. 67; IX.2.a, note ii, p. 95). The vocalization of the conjunction as וָ occurs with certain pairs of words, and it may also occur when the conjunction is immediately before certain accented syllables, such as תֹהוּ וָבֹ֫הוּ in Gen 1:2 (BDB, p. 251; Joüon, §104c, d, pp. 347–49).
2. Because all the men who were seeking your life have died
   Remember that the *dāgēš* in the second radical may be lost when followed by *šĕwāʾ* (XV.7, note, p. 177).
3. You have seen that I spoke with you from heaven.
4. The heavens tell/are telling the glory of God.
5. Just as YHWH commanded them, so they did.
6. Are you the man who spoke to the woman?
7. In God we have boasted all day.
8. You forgave (lit. "lifted") the iniquity of your people, you have covered all their sins (assuming collective, or "their every sin").
9. Many seek (the) face of the ruler, but the judgment of humanity is from YHWH.
   On the absence of the article in poetic Hebrew, see Excursus E, p. 157.
10. Now, this is the blessing (with) which Moses, the man of God, blessed the Israelites (sons of Israel) before his death.

15.d. Jer 45:1–5

v 1: דִּבֵּר Verbs ending in ר often have a *qiṭṭel* pattern in the Piel (XV.1.i, p. 173)—בְּכָתְבוֹ "when he wrote"—מִפִּי construct form of פֶּה

(XI.2.k, p. 121, noun list; looks just like the noun form with 1cs suffix; see XII.2.e, p. 140) + prefixed preposition מִן: "from the mouth of." The chain is definite because the absolute is a proper name. Remember that a noun is definite if (1) it has a definite article, (2) is a proper name, or (3) has a pronominal suffix (IX.3.a, p. 98)—בַּשָּׁנָה הָרְבִעִית "in the fourth year"—לֵאמֹר literally, "saying," but it is best left untranslated here.

v 3: אוֹי־נָא "woe."

v 4: תֹּאמַר "you shall say"—הִיא is odd; we would expect הַהִיא (X.I, p. 105).

v 5: תְּבַקֶּשׁ־לְךָ "will you seek (object) for yourself"—גְדֹלוֹת substantive use of the adjective (VII.3.c, p. 72); the fem. form, singular or plural, is often used for semantic neuters (VII.4.c, p. 73)—אַל־תְּבַקֵּשׁ "do not seek"—הִנְנִי particle הִנֵּה + 1cs suffix (IX.5, pp. 99–100)—מֵבִיא "I am bringing"—וְנָתַתִּי "and I will give"—תֵּלֶךְ־שָׁם lit.: "you shall go there."

Review the Concepts

Write the Piel perfect form of the following verbs and translate:

1. הָלַל 1cp
2. כָּלָה 3fs
3. יָלַד fp participle
4. מלא 3cp
5 מֵאֵן ms participle
6. בָּרַךְ 2mp
7. שָׁרַת mp participle

Answers

1. הִלַּלְתִּי I praised
2. כִּלְּתָה she finished
3. מְיַלְּדוֹת the ones begetting, or midwives
4. מִלְאוּ they filled (The *dāgēš* in the second radical may be lost when followed by *šewā*ʾ ["Sqnmlwy," VI.7, p. 59; XV.1, note ii, p. 173]).
5. מְמָאֵן one who refuses
6. בֵּרַכְתֶּם you blessed
7. מְשָׁרְתִים ones serving

Lesson 16

In This Lesson

1. The Hiphil Perfect: הִקְטִיל
2. The Meaning of Verbs in Hiphil
   causative, factitive, denominative, declarative
3. The Hiphil Perfect of I-Guttural Verbs
4. The Hiphil Perfect of III-Guttural Verbs
5. The Hiphil Perfect of III-*ʾÁlep̄* Verbs
   quiescent א (lesson II)
6. The Hiphil Perfect of III-*Hē* Verbs
7. The Hiphil Perfect of I-*Nûn* Verbs
   assimilated נ (lesson IV)
8. The Hiphil Perfect of I-*Wāw* Verbs
   contraction of diphthong **-aw-* > *-ô-* (lesson IV)
9. The Hiphil Perfect of I-*Yōḏ* Verbs
   contraction of diphthong **-ay-* > *-ê-* (lesson IV)
10. The Hiphil Perfect of II-*Wāw/Yōḏ* Verbs
11. Hiphil Verbs as Causatives
12. The Hiphil Participle

Terms to Know

causative
declarative (XV)
denominative (XV)
diphthong, contraction of (IV)
factitive (XV)
perfect (XIII)

Tips

1. Some students find it helpful to know that an older form of the Hiphil prefix was **ha-* (rather than *hi-*). This elucidates many perfect forms and the Hiphil participles.

2. Like many forms, the Hiphil perfect of I-*Wāw* and I-*Yōḏ* verbs are more easily understood if one briefly reviews the contraction of unstressed diphthongs **-aw-* and **-ay-* (IV.2.c.iii.β, p. 28; IV.2.c.iv.β, p. 29).

3. The Hiphil shares certain usages already learned with the Piel (factitive, denominative, declarative). Do not worry yourself trying to anticipate which verbal roots will appear in the Piel or Hiphil: just take the Bible one verb at a time!

ANSWER KEY

16.a.

1. Hiphil perf. 3ms יָטַב to do well, please
   This form derives from **hayṭîḇ* (XVI.9, note, p. 186).

2. Hiphil perf. 1cs נָגַד Hi.: to tell, announce, report
   Observe assimilation of first radical: **hingáḏtî* (XVI.7, p. 184).

3. Hiphil perf. 2ms יָצָא to come out, to go forth
   With contraction of **haw-* to *hô-* (XVI.8.a, note, p. 185).

4. Qal perf. 2mp נָטַע to plant

5. Hiphil perf. 1cs נָכָה Hi.: to strike, smite, defeat
   Just as in Qal and Piel, a III-*Hē* root will, in Hiphil perfect first- and second-person verbs, be retained as *mater yôḏ*. See chart at XVI.6, p. 184.

6. Hiphil perf. 1cs נָחַל to inherit, possess; Hi.: to bequeath, assign inheritance

7. Hiphil perf. 1cp יָטַב to do well, please

8. Hiphil perf. 3cp נָגַד Hi.: to tell, announce, report

9. Qal perf. 3fs רָבָה to become great, numerous

10. Qal perf. 3cp רָבָה to become great, numerous
    There does exist a geminate biform of the root רָבָה (i.e., רָבַב). Geminate verbs will be treated in a later chapter.

11. Hiphil perf. 1cs רָבָה to become great, numerous

12. Piel perf. 3cp שָׁחַת Pi.: to ruin, destroy; Hi.: to ruin, destroy

13. Piel perf. 2ms רָבָה Pi.: to increase, bring up

14. Hiphil perf. 3cp שָׁחַת Pi.: to ruin, destroy; Hi.: to ruin, destroy

15. Qal act. ptc. mp צָעַק to cry out

16.b.

1. נָטַ֫עְתִּי

2. הִצִּיל
3. הִכָּה
4. הִכּוּ

   In the above three examples, note the assimilated I-*Nûn*. In 3 and 4, remember that afformatives may "conceal" a III-*Hē*.

5. הִשְׁלִיכָה
6. דֱּרְשָׁה
7. הִשְׁלִיכוּ
8. צָעֲקוּ
9. הוֹשַׁעְתָּ
10. הִגִּידָה
11. הָרַגְתָּ
12. שָׁתִית

16.c.

1. I declared and saved and proclaimed (caused to hear).
2. Now, these are the kings of the land whom the Israelites smote.
3. But he did not tell his father and his mother what he had done.

   The relative clause אֲשֶׁר עָשָׂה is implicitly definite, as one can see from the marker of the definite direct object אֵת (IX.3, p. 98; BDB I. אֵת 1.a, pp. 84–85).
4. He has told you, O mortal (human), what is good and what YHWH demands from you.
5. But YHWH cast upon them large stones from heaven.

   Observe that the adjective גְּדֹלוֹת agrees with the irregular feminine noun אֲבָנִים.
6. What is this you have done to me? Why have you not told me that she is your wife?

   For the function here of זֹּאת, see X.7.b, p. 111. The "conjunctive *dāgēš*" in לִּי is there for euphonic reasons (Excursus B.6, p. 69; also GKC, §20.c, p. 71).
7. You killed YHWH's people.

   In הֲמִתֶּם the final radical of מוּת assimilates into the 2mp afformative (see example in XVI.10, note ii, p. 187).

8. Why is YHWH bringing us to this land?

9. For I am YHWH your God, the holy one of Israel, your savior.
As a verbal adjective, the participle מוֹשִׁיעֶךָ may be used substantively (i.e., as a noun) and thus may take a pronominal suffix (VIII.4.c, p. 83; XII.1, pp. 132–33).

10. YHWH has brought you out by a strong hand.

11. But YHWH smote every firstborn in the land of Egypt.
Word order suggests this disjunctive translation of the initial ו (XIII.4.b, p. 150).

12. Now I myself am establishing my covenant with you and your seed after you.
For the translation "establish," see BDB קוּם 6.d, p. 879.

13. It is the word that I spoke to Pharaoh; what God is about to do he has shown Pharaoh.
עֹשֶׂה is translated here as a participle of incipient action (XIII.4.iii, p. 82). Note that in הֶרְאָה "he has shown," the Hiphil prefix -הֶ is like that of a guttural (XVI.3, p. 183), but the ר takes a normal silent *šěwāʾ* רְ instead of a composite *šěwāʾ* *רֱ. As we have seen, ר acts like a guttural in some ways but not in others.

14. This is the sign of the covenant that I have established between me and between all flesh that is on the earth.
For the translation "establish," see BDB קוּם 6.d, p. 879.

15. And they have not said, "Where is YHWH, the one who brought us up from the land of Egypt, the one who led us through the wilderness?"

16.d. 1 Kgs 8:12–21

v 12: אָמַר לִשְׁכֹּן "promised to dwell" (BDB אָמַר 3, p. 56).

v 13: בָּנֹה בָנִיתִי "I have indeed built"—לְשִׁבְתְּךָ "for you to dwell."

v 14: וַיַּסֵּב "then (subject) turned around"—פָּנָיו See BDB פָּנֶה p. 815—וַיְבָרֶךְ "and blessed"—וְכָל־קְהַל "while all the assembly of"; the disrupted word order suggests some such translation of ו (XIII.4.b, p. 150).

v 15: וַיֹּאמֶר "and he said."

v 16: לִבְנוֹת "to build"—לִהְיוֹת "for (subject) to be"—וָאֶבְחַר "and I chose"; the object of בָּחַר is usually indicated by the preposition בְּ (see XIV Vocabulary, p. 167)—לִהְיוֹת "to be."

v 17: וַיְהִי "now it was"—לִבְנוֹת "to build."

v 18: וַיֹּאמֶר "and (subject) said"—יַעַן אֲשֶׁר See X.8, p. 112; BDB יַעַן p. 774.

v 19: לֹא תִבְנֶה "you will not build"—כִּי אִם־ "but rather"—יִבְנֶה "will build."

v 20: וַיָּקֶם "and (subject) established"—וָאָקֻם "I have risen"—וָאֵשֵׁב "and I have sat"—וָאֶבְנֶה "and I have built."

v 21: וָאָשִׂם "and I have set"—בְּהוֹצִיאוֹ "when he brought out."

Review the Concepts

Translate the following (use BDB and your grammar) and attempt to describe the Hiphil verbs as causative, factitive, denominative, or declarative (XVI.2, pp. 181–83).

1. הִמְלַכְתִּי אֶת־שָׁאוּל לְמֶלֶךְ (1 Sam 15:11)
2. אָבִיךָ הִכְבִּיד אֶת־עֻלֵּנוּ (1 Kgs 12:10)
3. וְהִשְׁכַּמְתֶּם מָחָר לְדַרְכְּכֶם (Judg 19:9)
4. הִנֵּה הֶחֱיָה יְהוָה אוֹתִי כַּאֲשֶׁר דִּבֵּר (Josh 14:10)
5. מַצְדִּיק רָשָׁע וּמַרְשִׁיעַ צַדִּיק (Prov 17:15)
6. וְהֶעֱבִירוּ תַעַר עַל־כָּל־בְּשָׂרָם (Num 8:7)
7. כִּי לֹא הִמְטִיר יְהוָה אֱלֹהִים עַל־הָאָרֶץ (Gen 2:5)
8. קָרָאתִי לָךְ אִשָּׁה מֵינֶקֶת מִן הָעִבְרִיֹּת (Exod 2:7)
9. הִשְׁפַּלְתִּי עֵץ גָּבֹהַ (Ezek 17:24)
10. הֲלוֹא אַתְּ־הִיא הַמַּחְצֶבֶת רַהַב (Isa 51:9)

Answers

1. I have made Saul to rule as king. (causative, from מָלַךְ)
2. Your father has made our yoke heavy. (factitive, from stative verb כָּבֵד "be heavy")
3. Tomorrow you may rise early on your way. (denominative, from noun שְׁכֶם "shoulder")
4. See, YHWH has preserved me, just as he said. (factitive, from stative verb חָיָה "to live")

5. One acquitting the wicked and one condemning the righteous (both verbs are declarative; note that מַצְדִּיק is also denominative from the noun צֶדֶק)
6. They shall shave ("cause a razor to pass over") their entire body. (causative, from עָבַר)
7. For YHWH God had not made it rain upon the earth. (denominative, from noun מָטָר "rain")
8. Shall I summon for you a nursing ("causing to suckle") woman from among the Hebrews? (causative, from יָנַק)
9. I bring low the high tree (factitive, from stative verb שָׁפֵל "be low")
10. Was it not you who clove Rahab? (in this case, the Hiphil = the Qal: cleave or hew).

    N.B. These categories are useful tools, but many occurrences of the Hiphil will resist easy categorization. Let context be your guide.

Lesson 17

In This Lesson

1. The Perfect with Object Suffixes
   changes to the afformatives
   changes before the afformatives
   forms of the object suffixes
2. The Perfect of III-*Hē* Verbs with Suffixes
   regular for their type, except the 3ms and 3fs forms
3. Irregular Vocalization
4. Redundant Object Suffix

Terms to Know

afformative (XIII)
direct object (IX)
full and defective spelling (II)
verbal patterns (VIII)

Tips

1. Changes to the perfect afformatives before suffixes: (a) 3fs ָה- becomes ַת-/ָת-; (b) 2ms תָּ becomes תּ; (c) 2fs תְּ becomes תִּי/תִּ (identical to the 1cs; defective spelling is not uncommon); (d) 2mp/2fp תֶּם/תֶּן both become תּוּ/תֻּ

2. When object suffixes are added to the perfect, it becomes easy to confuse the 3fs, the 2ms, and the 2fs afformatives, all marked by ת. Distinguish these afformatives with suffixes by noting the following: (a) the 3fs afformative with suffixes is preceded by an *a*-vowel; (b) the 2ms afformative with suffixes is preceded by a silent *šĕwāʾ* in the strong verb; (c) the 2fs afformative with suffixes will have *ḥîreq-yōḏ* or *ḥîreq*.

Answer Key

17.a.

1. Piel perf. 1cs/2fs צִוָּה + obj. sfx. 3ms to command
   The 1cs and 2fs afformatives with suffixed pronouns are identical (XVII.1.a.iii, note γ, p. 194).

2. Qal perf. 3ms שָׁלַח + obj. sfx. 3ms to send
3. Piel perf. 1cs/2fs כָּלָה + obj. sfx. 3mp to complete
The Piel perfect of כָּלָה may take a *ḥîreq-yōḏ* or a *ṣērê-yōḏ* with the second radical.
4. Qal perf. 3ms אָהַב + obj. sfx. 3ms to love
The *ṣērê* is irregular, so too in nos. 13 and 15 below (XVII.3, p. 200).
5. Piel perf. 3ms כָּלָה + obj. sfx. 3mp to complete
6. Qal perf. 3ms סָפַר + obj. sfx. 3mp to count
7. Qal perf. 3fs הָרַג + obj. sfx. 3mp to kill
8. Piel perf. 3fs צָוָה + obj. sfx. 3fs to command
9. Piel perf. 2ms כָּלָה + obj. sfx. 3mp to complete
10. Piel perf. 3ms צָוָה + obj. sfx. 3mp to command
11. Piel perf. 2ms קָדַשׁ + obj. sfx. 3ms to be holy
12. Piel perf. 3fs כָּלָה + obj. sfx. 3ms to complete
The 3ms object suffix with the 2fs perfect can be תּוּ as well as הוּ- (XVII.1.d, note i, p. 197).
13. Qal perf. 3fs אָהַב + obj. sfx. 3ms to love
14. Hiphil perf. 1cs קָדַשׁ + obj. sfx. 2ms to be holy
The 2fs subject would not make sense with the 2ms object suffix.
15. Qal perf. 3cp אָהַב + obj. sfx. 3mp to love

17.b.

1. שְׂנֵאתִ֫יו
2. הֲרָגַ֫נִי
3. אֲהַבְתִּ֫יךָ
4. עָנָם
5. צִוִּיתִ֫יךָ
6. שְׂנֵאתִ֫ים
7. שְׁכַחְתַּ֫נִי
8. הִלְלוּךָ
The first ל loses the expected strong *dāḡēš* as a "Sqnmlwy" letter (VI.7, p. 59; XV.7, note, p. 177). The *šěwā᾽* is vocal (see II.6.b.iii, p. 10, n. 2).

9. הֲרַגְתִּ֫יךָ

10. צִוִּיתָ֫נוּ

17.c.

1. My people have forgotten me.
   The *ṣērê* is irregular (XVII.3, p. 200). The 3cp perfect afformative is spelled defectively, ֻ instead of וּ. The verb is plural because עַם is a collective (XIII.4.c, note i, p. 151).

2. Their fathers taught them.
   אָבוֹת is an irregular plural (V.3, p. 43).

3. Today I have begotten you.
   For this irregular vocalization of the *qāṭal* Qal perfect, see XVII.3, p. 200.

4. He clothed me with garments of salvation.

5. And I have not learned wisdom.

6. All who found them have devoured them.
   מוֹצְאֵיהֶם is a substantive Qal act. ptc. in construct + pronominal sfx. For the participle in construct, see XI.2.c, p. 118; XI.3, pp. 121–22.

7. He brought me to the house of wine.

8. An evil creature devoured him.

9. My God, my God, why have you abandoned me?
   For the interrogative particle לָ֫מָּה, see X.6.d, p. 110.

10. I knew you in the wilderness.

17.d.

1. You hate me, and you do not love me.
   For the translation of the perfect here, review XIII.3.c, p.148.

2. Why have you brought us up from Egypt?
   The 2mp afformative is usually spelled defectively before the object suffix (XVII.1.a.iv, p. 194).

3. Surely YHWH your God blessed you in all the work of your hand.
   For the translation of כִּי, review X Vocabulary, p. 113.

4. I taught you statutes and judgments just as YHWH my God commanded me.
   In the 3ms perfect of III-*Hē* verbs the final weak radical is lost before the object suffix (XVII.2.b, p. 200).

5. (The) day when my mother bore me
6. I did not speak with your fathers, and I did not command them.
   On identifying the use of אֶת־ here, review IX.3.a, note, p. 98.
7. God appointed me lord over all of Egypt
   For שִׂים + לְ, see BDB שִׂים 3.d, pp. 963–64; see also BDB לְ 4, p. 512.
   For the second לְ, see BDB לְ 5, p. 512.
8. The king saved us from the hand of our enemies.
   For the Hiphil perfect of I-*Nûn* verbs, see XVI.7, p. 184.
9. Indeed, the hate with which he hated her was greater than the love with which he had loved her.
10. I anointed you as king over Israel, and I rescued you from the hand of Saul.
11. But you did not incline your ear, and you did not listen to me.
12. He commanded me, and he placed all these words in the mouth of your maidservant.
13. (As for this) Moses, the man who brought us up from the land of Egypt, we do not know what has happened to him.
14. I am YHWH your God who (I) brought you from the land of Egypt, from a house of slaves.
15. David did what was right in the eyes of YHWH, and he did not turn from all that he commanded him all the days of his life.
    For translation of יָשָׁר, see BDB יָשָׁר 2.a, p. 449.

17.e. Song 3:1–5

v 1: For the relative particle שֶׁ־, see X.2.b, pp. 106–7.

v 2: אָקוּמָה נָּא וַאֲסוֹבְבָה "I will rise and roam about"—אֲבַקְשָׁה "I will seek."

v 3: For the unmarked interrogative here, see X.6.a, p. 109.

v 4: For כִּמְעַט, see BDB מְעַט 2.a, p. 590—For the preposition שֶׁ־ + עַד, see BDB III. עַד II.1.a, pp. 724–25; here and in v 5 שֶׁ־ is attached to a finite verb—וְלֹא אַרְפֶּנּוּ "and I will not let him go"—הוֹרָתִי Qal act. ptc. fs of הָרָה (to conceive) + 1cs pronominal sfx.

v 5: אִם־תָּעִירוּ "do not stir"—וְאִם־תְּעוֹרְרוּ "and do not rouse"—עַד שֶׁתֶּחְפָּץ "until it please."

Review the Concepts

Multiple Choice: Translate:

1. עָנָךְ
   a. they answered me
   b. he answered you (ms)
   c. he answered you (fs)
   d. she answered him
2. שְׁאֵל֫וּנוּ
   a. they asked us
   b. she asked him
   c. they asked me
   d. they asked him
3. מִלְטֵ֫נוּ
   a. we saved him
   b. she saved us
   c. he saved her
   d. he saved us
4. עָנַנִי
   a. I answered
   b. she answered
   c. he answered me
   d. she answered him
5. כִּבַּדְתַּ֫נִי
   a. I am honored
   b. you (ms) are heavy
   c. you (ms) honored me
   d. she honored me
6. צִוַּ֫תָּה
   a. he commanded her
   b. she commanded her
   c. you (fs) commanded it
   d. she commanded him
7. נְטַעְתָּם
   a. she planted them
   b. you (fs) stretched them out
   c. you (fs) planted them
   d. you (ms) planted them

Answers

1. c
2. a
3. d
4. c
5. c
6. b
7. d

Lesson 18

In This Lesson

1. The Imperfect Inflection
   marked by afformatives and preformatives; see chart (XVIII.1, p. 205)
2. The Qal Imperfect
   dynamic typically יִשְׁמֹר
   stative typically יִכְבַּד
   see chart for patterns (XVIII.2, p. 206).
3. The Uses of the Imperfect
   future
   custom
   modal ("should," etc.)
   with particles טֶ֫רֶם ("not yet, before") and עַד ("until")
4. Expressions of Will
   cohortative (first person): "let me…," "let us…" (usually has final ָה -)
   jussive (third person): "let him…," "may she…," etc.
   command (second person): "may you…"
5. Negation of Imperfects, Jussives, and Cohortatives
   לֹא (general prohibition), אַל (specific action)
6. The נָא Particle

Terms to Know

afformative (XIII)
cohortative
dynamic (XIII)
jussive
preformative
stative (XIII)
thematic vowel

Tips

1. The perfect is marked by an afformative. The imperfect, by contrast, is marked by a preformative, in some cases also taking an afformative. Look first for these preformatives (י, ת, נ, or א) when identifying the imperfect.

2. When learning the imperfect preformatives and afformatives, study the chart (XVIII.1, p. 205) and note the distinguishing markers.

(a) י preformative: 3ms and 3mp forms
(b) א and נ preformative: 1cs and 1cp forms
(c) וּ afformative: 3mp and 2mp forms
(d) נָה afformative: 3fp and 2fp forms
(e) י afformative: 2fs

3. For the strong verb, the jussive looks identical to the imperfect form, so context will be the only indicator that a form is jussive. This is also true for second-person imperfect forms that function as a command.

4. The second-person jussive, though it may function as a command (XVIII.4.c, p. 209), differs in form from the second-person commands expressed in the imperative (the imperative will be introduced in lesson XXI). To distinguish these two forms, it is helpful to translate second-person jussives as "may you. . . ."

Answer Key

18.a.

1. Qal impf. 1cs כָּתַב to write
2. Qal impf. 3ms שָׁאַל to ask
3. Qal impf. 3ms בָּחַר to choose
4. Qal impf. 1cp כָּרַת to cut
5. Qal impf. 3ms מָשַׁח to anoint
6. Qal impf. 2mp כָּתַב to write
7. Qal impf. 3mp שָׁכַב to lie down
8. Qal impf. 2fs זָכַר to remember
9. Qal impf. 2mp כָּרַת to cut
10. Qal impf. 1cp דָּרַשׁ to seek
11. Qal impf. 3mp מָשַׁח to anoint
12. Qal impf. 2/3fp שָׁמַע to hear
13. Qal impf. 2fs בָּטַח to trust
14. Qal impf. (cohortative) 1cs זָבַח to sacrifice
15. Qal impf. 3/2fp שָׁלַח to send

18.b.

1. תִּשְׁמְרִי

2. תִּשְׁאַל
3. יִמְשֹׁל
4. אֶשְׁכַּב
5. נִזְבְּחָה
6. אֶשְׁלְחָה
7. יִזְכֹּר
8. לֹא אֶשְׁמַע אֲלֵיהֶם
9. אַל תִּשְׁלַח אֶת־יָדְךָ
   For translation, see tip 4.
10. לֹא תִזְבַּח

18.c.

1. Who may dwell on your holy mountain?
2. He will remember his covenant forever.
3. I will rejoice in YHWH.
4. He will lie with you tonight.
5. Shall a man like me flee?
6. By me kings (shall) reign.
7. He will send his messenger.
8. Let us send men.
9. Whom shall I send?
10. Do not send! (2fp)
11. I will pursue my enemies.
12. We will cut trees.

18.d.

1. You will reign over Israel.
2. To you I will sacrifice a sacrifice of thanksgiving.
3. I will make (lit., "cut") with you an everlasting covenant.
   The final ָה - usually marks the cohortative, but it sometimes appears with various forms of the imperfect without any particular significance (XVIII.4.a, note, p. 208).

4. There they will make sacrifices of righteousness.
   Literally, "they will sacrifice sacrifices." When the verb and object are derived from the same root, this is called an internal or cognate accusative (GKC, §117p, p. 366).

5. Our God, will you not execute judgment against them?
   For the translation "execute judgment," see BDB שָׁפַט 3, p. 1047; for the translation "against," see BDB בְּ 4.a, p. 89.

6. Your ears will hear a word from behind you, saying, "This is the way."
   Note that "ears" takes a feminine verb. Parts of the body that come in pairs tend to be feminine (III.1.b.v, note, p. 18).

7. Lest we burn you and your father's house with fire.

8. Who is YHWH that I should obey his voice?

9. I will not rule over you, and my son will not rule over you; YHWH will rule over you.

10. For this is the covenant that I will make (literally: "cut") with the house of Israel.

18.e. Deut 13:1–6

v 1: לַעֲשׂוֹת "to do"—לֹא־תֹסֵף "you shall not add."

v 2: יָקוּם Qal impf. 3ms of קוּם—וְנָתַן "and he gives."

v 3: וּבָא "and (subject) comes" (i.e., "comes to pass")—נֵלְכָה Qal coh. 1cp of הָלַךְ—יְדַעְתָּם contains a redundant object suffix that does not need to be translated in English (XVII.4, p. 201)—וְנָעָבְדֵם "and let us serve them."

v 4: לָדַעַת "to know"—הֲיִשְׁכֶם = הֲ (interrogative particle) + יֵשׁ + pronominal suffix (X.3.b, p. 107).

v 5: תֵּלֵכוּ Qal impf 2mp of הָלַךְ—תִירָאוּ Qal impf. 2mp of יָרֵא—תַעֲבֹדוּ Qal impf. 2mp of עָבַד—תִדְבָּקוּן Remember that the 3mp and 2mp forms of the Qal impf. frequently have an additional ן at the end (XVIII.1, note ii, p. 205).

v 6: יוּמָת "shall be put to death"—וְהַפֹּדְךָ Qal ptc. + obj. sfx.—לְהַדִּיחֲךָ "to divert you"—לָלֶכֶת "to walk"—וּבִעַרְתָּ "so you shall purge."

REVIEW THE CONCEPTS

Indicate the possible translation(s) for the following phrases, keeping in mind the imperfect aspect.

1. יִשְׂרֹף הַהֵיכָל

a. He may burn the palace.

b. Let him burn the palace.

c. He had to burn the palace.

2. הַנָּשִׁים תִּקְבֹּרְנָה הָאֲנָשִׁים

a. Did the women bury the men?

b. The men will bury the women.

c. The women used to bury the men.

3. לֹא אֶקְבֹּץ לֶחֶם

a. Let me gather food.

b. I will not gather food.

c. Do not gather food.

4. לֹא יִרְדְּפוּ אֹתִי

a. I did not pursue them.

b. They would not pursue me.

c. Let them not pursue me.

5. יִשְׁפְּכוּן מַיִם

a. They (cp) used to pour out water.

b. They (fp) used to pour out water.

c. They (mp) used to pour out water.

Answers

1. a, b
2. c
3. b
4. b, c
5. c

Lesson 19

In This Lesson

1. The Qal Imperfect of I-Guttural Verbs
2. The Qal Imperfect of III-*ʾÁlep̄* Verbs
   quiescent א (lesson II)
3. The Qal Imperfect of III-*Hē* Verbs
4. The Qal Imperfect of I-*Nûn* Verbs
   assimilated נ (lesson IV)
   לָקַח often belongs also to this inflection.
5. The Qal Imperfect of I-*Wāw* Verbs
   הָלַךְ often belongs also to this inflection.
6. The Qal Imperfect of I-*Yōḏ* Verbs
7. The Qal Imperfect of II-*Wāw/Yōḏ* Verbs
8. The Verb יָכֹל

Terms to Know

composite *šĕwāʾ* (II)
defective spelling of *matres* (II)
imperfect inflection (XVIII)
méṯeḡ (Excursus B)
preformative (XVIII)
quiescent א (II)

Tips

1. Much like lesson XIV, this lesson simply adds the behavior of "weak" roots to an inflection you have already learned. Although the lesson appears to have a lot of detail, there is little here that is truly new. Take your time and try to make sense of the several inflections charted in this lesson.

2. A brief review of the imperfect inflection of the strong verb (lesson XVIII) may be helpful before working in this lesson with the "weak" roots.

3. For some weak roots in the imperfect inflection, the vowel under the preformative may offer a helpful "field mark" to the root.

(a) I-*Wāw:* the preformative has *ṣērê*, as in יֵשֵׁב.

(b) II-*Wāw/Yōḏ:* the preformative has *qāmeṣ*, as in יָקוּם.

ANSWER KEY

19.a.

1. Qal impf. 3ms אָחַז to seize
I-*ʾĀlep̄* verbs of the אָכַל type (XIX.1.c, p. 214) often have *ē* instead of *a* as the thematic vowel (XIX.1.d, note ii, p. 215).

2. Qal impf. 1cp לָקַח to take
לָקַח behaves like a I-*Nûn* root in Qal impf. (XIX.4.d, p. 217).

3. Qal impf. 2ms/3fs אָבָה to be willing

4. Qal impf. 1cs חָדַל to cease

5. Qal impf. 3ms אָסַר to bind

6. Qal impf. 1cs יָכֹל to be able
For the unique inflection of this verb, see XIX.8, p. 220.

7. Qal impf. 2fs יָשַׁב to sit
The *ṣērê* under the preformative is a helpful "field mark" of the Qal impf. I-*Wāw* verb (XIX.5.a.iii, p. 217; chart XIX.5.b, p. 218). Recall that all originally I-*Wāw* roots appear in your dictionary as I-*Yōḏ* (IV.2.c.i, pp. 27–28).

8. Qal impf. 1cs יָדַע to know

9. Qal impf. 3ms חָלַק to divide

10. Qal impf. 3mp חָפֵץ to desire, delight

11. Qal impf. 3mp יָרַשׁ to possess

12. Qal impf. 2mp חָלַק to divide, apportion

13. Qal impf. 3mp נָסַע to set out
One may expect יִסְּעוּ, with doubling of the ס showing an assimilated I-*Nûn*. However, recall that the strong *dāḡēš* may be lost when the "Sqnmlwy" consonants take a *šĕwāʾ* (VI.7, p. 59; XIX.4.d, note, p. 217).

14. Qal impf. 1cp בּוֹא to enter

15. Qal impf. 2fs יָרֵא to fear

16. Qal impf. (cohortative) 1cp הָלַךְ to go
This verb behaves like I-*Wāw* in Qal and Hiphil impf. (XIX.5.c, p. 218). Also, to review cohortatives, see XVIII.4.a, p. 208.

17. Qal impf. 1cp חָדַל to cease

18. Qal impf. 3mp חָשַׁב to plot
For an explanation of the final ן, see XVIII.1, note ii, p. 205.

19. Qal impf. 2fs נָתַן to give

20. Qal impf. (cohortative) 1cs סוּר to turn aside

21. Qal impf. 3mp נָפַל to fall

22. Qal impf. (cohortative) 1cs נוּס to flee

23. Qal impf. 2/3fp בּוֹא to enter

24. Qal impf. 3mp לָקַח to take
As noted previously, לָקַח behaves like a I-*Nûn* root in Qal impf. (XIX.4.d, p. 217). Note again also the loss of the strong *dāgēš* after a "Sqnmlwy" letter (VI.7, p. 59; XIX.4.d, note, p. 217).

19.b.

1. נִבְנֶה
2. נְרוּצָה
With propretonic reduction of the expected *qā́meṣ* (III.2.a.i, p. 20).
3. נוּכַל
4. נִירַשׁ
5. אֹמַר
This spelling derives from *אֹאמַר (see XIX.1.d, note iii, p. 215).
6. אֶתֵּן
7. אֵלֵךְ or אֶהֱלֹךְ
See XIX.5.c, p. 218.
8. אֶקַּח
9. תִּירְשׁוּ
10. יִהְיוּ
11. יָנ֫וּסוּ
12. תֹּאמַ֫רְנָה
13. תּוּכְלִי
14. יַעַמְדוּ
15. תַּעֲמֹ֫דְנָה
16. יֹאבֶה

19.c.

1. Instruction will not perish from (the) priest, nor counsel from (the) wise, nor word from (the) prophet.

2. We shall take their daughters for ourselves as wives, and we will give our daughters to them.
   Or "Let us take..." The cohortative is usually marked by הָ- but sometimes must (like the jussive) be inferred from context (XVIII.4.a, p. 208).

3. I trust in God; I am not afraid. What can a human do to me?

4. Will they fall and not arise again? Will they turn (away), and not turn (back)?

5. Let us arise and go, and we will live and not die.
   Or "that we might live and not die." Such "purpose clauses" will be examined in lesson XXI.

6. In this house and in Jerusalem, which I have chosen from all the tribes of Israel, I will set my name forever.
   Everything up through יִשְׂרָאֵל is an adverbial clause preceding the main verb. Where did God set God's name forever? "In this house ..." (See Normal Word Order, XIII.4.a.i, p. 149.)

7. Afterwards, the Israelites would depart, and in (the) place where the cloud would settle, there the Israelites would camp.
   Note the loss of the strong *dāgēš* in the ס of יִסְעוּ; see VI.7, p. 59; XIX.4.d, note, p. 217. For the construct form בִּמְקוֹם, see XIII.7.b, p. 153. For the *qāmeṣ ḥāṭûp* in יִשְׁכָּן, see XVIII.2, note ii, p. 207.

8. Now, my daughter, do not fear. I will do all that you say, because all of the gate of my people knows that you are a woman of substance.
   שַׁ֫עַר functions as a metonym for "those sitting within the gate"; see BDB I. שַׁ֫עַר 2.a, p. 1045.

9. He shall be for you as a mouth, and you shall be for him as God. Take this staff in your hand with which you will perform the signs.

10. If you should give to me half of your house, I will not go with you, nor will I eat food or drink water in this place. For thus he commanded me by the word of YHWH, saying, "You shall not eat food or drink water or return by the way that you came."
    For עִמָּךְ, see IX.2.a, note ii, p. 95. For the translation of צִוָּה in an impersonal construction, see XIV.7.a, p. 166.

19.d. Exod 3:1–14

v 1: The initial וְ is disjunctive (XIII.4.b, p. 150)—וַיִּנְהַג "and he drove"—וַיָּבֹא "and he came"—חֹרֵבָה note the unaccented ה ָ- (XIII.6, p. 152).

v 2: וַיֵּרָא "(subject) appeared"—בְּלַבַּת See BDB לַבָּה p. 526, which leads you to BDB לַהַב p. 529—וַיַּרְא "and he saw"—אֵינֶנּוּ See X.5.a, p. 108—אֻכָּל "consumed."

v 3: וַיֹּאמֶר "(subject) said"—אָסֻרָה־נָּא To parse and translate, see XIX.7, pp. 219–20; XVIII.4.a, p. 208; XVIII.6, p. 210—וְאֶרְאֶה "and I will see."

v 4: וַיַּרְא "(subject) saw"—לִרְאוֹת "to see"—וַיִּקְרָא "and (subject) called"—וַיֹּאמֶר "and he said."

v 5: שַׁל "remove"—עָלָיו ... הַמָּקוֹם For the resumptive pronoun, see X.2.a, p. 106.

v 6: וַיַּסְתֵּר "(subject) hid"—מֵהַבִּיט "to look" (lit. "from looking").

v 7: רָאֹה רָאִיתִי "I have indeed seen."

v 8: וָאֵרֵד "I have descended"—לְהַצִּילוֹ "to rescue them"—וּלְהַעֲלֹתוֹ "and to bring them up"—הַהִוא For this form, see IX.1.a, note ii, p. 92; for its translation, see IX.1.b.iii, p. 93—זָבַת חָלָב To translate, see XI.3.a and XI.4, p. 122.

v 9: Although בָּאָה is accented as Qal perf. 3fs, its word order suggests an original participle (XIV.4, notes ii–iii, p. 163).

v 10: לְכָה וְאֶשְׁלָחֲךָ "come, let me send you"—וְהוֹצֵא "bring out."

v 11: אוֹצִיא "I should bring out."

v 12: עִמָּךְ See IX.2.a, note ii, p. 95—בְּהוֹצִיאֲךָ "when you bring out"—תַּעַבְדוּן For this form's additional ן, see XVIII.1, note ii, p. 205.

v 13: בָא is a participle, not a perfect verb (XIV.4, note ii, p. 163)—וְאָמַרְתִּי "and I will say"—וְאָמְרוּ "and they will say."

Review the Concepts

Vocabulary Acrostic! First, produce the forms described below, using vocabulary words from this lesson. Then solve the acrostic puzzle resulting from the answers, using the first consonant from each line (hint: a famous quote from Exod 3:1–14).

1. Qal impf. 1cs of root meaning "to run"

2. Hi. perf. 3ms of root meaning "to approach"
3. Qal impf. 3mp of root meaning "to be able"
4. Hi. perf. 3fs of root meaning "to flee"
5. Qal impf. 1cs of root meaning "to bind"
6. Masculine plural noun meaning "rods, tribes"
7. Qal perf. 3cp of root meaning "to run"
8. Qal perf. 3ms of root meaning "to seize"
9. Hi. perf. 1cs of root meaning "to possess"
10. Qal impf. 3mp of root meaning "to set out"
11. Definite noun meaning "the gates"

Answers

1. אָרוּץ
2. הִקְרִיב
3. יוּכְלוּ
4. הֵנִ֫יסָה
5. אֶאֱסַר
6. שְׁבָטִים
7. רָ֫צוּ
8. אָחַז
9. הוֹרַ֫שְׁתִּי
10. יִסְעוּ
11. הַשְּׁעָרִים

Solution to acrostic: see Exod 3:14: אֶהְיֶה אֲשֶׁר אֶהְיֶה

For other Bible acrostics, see, for example, Pss 25 and 34. (There are still others!)

Lesson 20

In This Lesson

1. The Preterite
   preterite use of *yiqṭōl*
2. Discourse on Past Situations
   qāṭal + *wayyiqṭōl* sequence
   vocalization of ו with consecutive forms
3. Discourse on Future Situations
   the *yiqṭōl* + *wĕqāṭal* sequence
   wĕqāṭal after a participle
4. The *Wāw*-Consecutive Forms: strong verb וַיִּקְטֹל; weak roots
5. Narrative Contexts
   past events
   future events
6. Concomitant Circumstances

Terms to Know

accent (retraction of)
apocope
consecutive perfect = *wĕqāṭal*
preterite
Wāw-consecutive = *wayyiqṭōl*
wĕyiqṭōl
yiqṭōl (XVIII)

Tips

1. *Wayyiqṭōl* forms have ו + doubling of the preformative.
2. *Wayyiqṭōl* forms always have an *a*-vowel with ו.
3. Since the *wayyiqṭōl* form for most verbs is similar to that of the imperfect, remember these general rules for identifying weak roots:
   (a) *ṣērê* as vowel of the preformative probably indicates I-*Wāw* root
   (b) *qāmeṣ* as vowel of the preformative probably indicates II-*Wāw*/*Yōḏ* root
4. *Wayyiqṭōl* forms should be translated with the past tense. Although the *wayyiqṭōl* form is often called *Wāw*-consecutive, it does not need to follow a perfect verb to refer to a past situation.

ANSWER KEY

20.a.

1. Qal *wayyiqṭōl* 2fs זָנָה to act like a prostitute, be promiscuous
2. Qal *wayyiqṭōl* 3ms יָשַׁב to dwell, sit, remain (contrast the form with no. 12 below)
   I-*Wāw* forms without endings show retraction of the accent and shortening of the final vowel (XX.4.b, p. 228).
3. Qal *wayyiqṭōl* 3ms הָלַךְ to walk, to go
   Recall that הָלַךְ behaves like a I-*Wāw* verb (XX.4.b, note, p. 228).
4. Qal *wayyiqṭōl* 3ms לָקַח to receive, take
   לָקַח behaves like a I-*Nûn* verb (XIX.4.d, p. 217).
5. Qal *wayyiqṭōl* 3ms הָיָה to be, come to pass, come about, happen
   This form is peculiar and occurs frequently; it should be memorized (XX.4.d, p. 230).
6. Qal *wayyiqṭōl* 2ms/3fs הָלַךְ to walk, to go
7. Qal *wayyiqṭōl* 3ms יָדַע to know
   יָדַע is a I-*Wāw*, III-Guttural verb with the expected retraction of the accent in the *wayyiqṭōl* form (XX.4.b, p. 228).
8. Qal *wayyiqṭōl* 3ms בָּכָה to weep
   Some III-*Hē* verbs have *ṣērê* in the preformative and no *sĕḡōl* inserted (XX.4.d, pp. 229–30).
9. Qal *wayyiqṭōl* 2ms/3fs חָזָה to see
   חָזָה is a III-*Hē*, I-Guttural verb with the expected apocope of ה and *páṯaḥ* inserted instead of *sĕḡōl* (XX.4.d, pp. 229–30).
10. Qal *wayyiqṭōl* 3ms בָּנָה to build
    This form has all three characteristics of III-*Hē* forms: apocope of ה, *sĕḡōl,* and retraction of the accent (XX.4.d, p. 229).
11. Qal *wayyiqṭōl* 3ms עָנָה to answer
12. Qal *wayyiqṭōl* 3ms שׁוּב to turn, to return (contrast the form with no. 2 above)
    II-*Wāw* verbs without endings generally show retraction of the accent and shortening of *šûreq* to *qāmeṣ ḥāṭûp̄* 4 (XX.4.c, pp. 228–29).
13. Qal *wayyiqṭōl* 3ms סוּר to turn aside
    A few II-*Wāw,* III-Guttural verbs show a retraction of the accent, but the final vowel is shortened to *páṯaḥ*, not to *ḥōlem* or *sĕḡōl* (XX.4.c, p. 229).

14. Qal *wayyiqṭōl* 3ms רָאָה to see
This form occurs very frequently and should be memorized (XX.4.d, p. 231).

15. Qal *wayyiqṭōl* 3ms עָשָׂה to make, to do

16. Qal *wayyiqṭōl* 1cp שׁוּב to turn, to return

17. Qal *wayyiqṭōl* 1cs אָכַל to eat, devour
The 1cs *wayyiqṭōl* of this verb is the same as the imperfect, with merging of the א (XIX.1.d, note iii, p. 215). The 1cs *wayyiqṭōl* of אָכַל is attested as וָאֹכַל and as the form here, וָאֹכֵל. The latter form is a pausal form (Gen 3:12, 13; Excursus B.5, p. 67). There is also compensatory lengthening in וָ before א (XX.2.b.iii, p. 226).

18. Qal *wayyiqṭōl* 2/3fp אָבַד to perish

19. Qal *wayyiqṭōl* 2/3fp זָנָה to act like a prostitute, be promiscuous

20. Qal *wayyiqṭōl* 1cs יָרֵא to fear, to be afraid
יָרֵא, though original I-*Wāw*, behaves like an original I-*Yōḏ* verb (XIX.6, p. 219) with compensatory lengthening in וָ before א (XX.2.b.iii, p. 226).

20.b.

1. וַיִּמְאַס

2. וַתִּגַּע
Review XIX.4.a, p. 216.

3. וַיָּצָם

4. וַתֵּלֶךְ

5. וַנָּבֹא

6. וַתֵּרֶא

7. וַתֵּשֶׁב

8. וַיִּירָא

9. וַיַּרְא
See XX.4.d, p. 231.

10. וָאֶקַּח
Review XIX.4.d, p. 217.

11. וַיָּמָת
See XX.4.c, pp. 228–29.

12. וַתָּבֹא

13. וַתֹּאמֶר
See XX.4.a, p. 228.

14. וַיִּתֵּן
Review XIX.4.b, p. 216.

15. וַיַּעַל
See XX.4.d, pp. 229–30.

16. וַיִּחַן
See XX.4.d, p. 230.

20.c. Gen 22:1–15

v 1: For the translation of הִנֵּנִי, see IX.5.b, p. 100.

v 2: קַח־נָא "take!"—וְלֶךְ־לְךָ "go!"—וְהַעֲלֵהוּ "and offer him up!"—אָהַבְתָּ For the translation, see XIII.3.c, p. 148—אַחַד "one of"—אֹמַר For the form, see XIX.1.d, note iii, p. 215.

v 3: וַיַּשְׁכֵּם "(subject) got up early"—אֶת־שְׁנֵי "two of"—וַיְבַקַּע "he split"—On the translation of the construct chain עֲצֵי עֹלָה, see XI.4, p. 122.

v 4: הַשְּׁלִישִׁי is the ordinal number "third" functioning as an attributive adjective.

v 5: שְׁבוּ־לָכֶם "you stay!"—וְנִשְׁתַּחֲוֶה "and we will worship."

v 7: The vocalization of הִנֶּנִּי with *sĕgōl* instead of *ṣērê* (cf. 22:1) occurs only here and in Gen 27:18 (Joüon, §102k, pp. 333–34)—For translation of הִנֵּה, see IX.5.b, p. 100—On the translation of וְ in וְאַיֵּה as disjunctive, see XIII.4.b, p. 150.

v 8: שְׁנֵיהֶם "the two of them"—For the translation of רָאָה here and in v 14, see BDB, רָאָה 6.g, p. 907.

v 9: For מִמַּעַל, see BDB II. מַעַל 1.b, p. 751.

v 10: לִשְׁחֹט "to slay."

v 12: On the form and use of יְרֵא, see XIV.5, p. 165.

v 13: נֶאֱחַז "caught"—וַיַּעֲלֵהוּ "and offered it up"—Many translations (NRSV, NIV, NJPS) follow the textual variant אֶחָד "a (one)" instead of MT's אַחַר "behind."

v 14: יֵאָמֵר "it is said"—יֵרָאֶה "it will be seen."

v 15: שֵׁנִית "a second time."

REVIEW THE CONCEPTS

Match each *wayyiqṭōl* form with the correct translation.

1. וַתִּשֶּׂ֫אנָה	a. she drank
2. וַתֵּ֫כֶל	b. he ran
3. וַיָּ֫נָס	c. it (fs) was great
4. וַתֵּ֫רֶא	d. it (fs) was complete
5. וַתֵּ֫רֶב	e. they (fp) lifted
6. וַתֵּט	f. it (ms) became great
7. וַיָּ֫רָץ	g. he fled
8. וַתֵּ֫שְׁתְּ	h. you (ms) stretched out
9. וָאֵשֵׁב	i. I dwelled
10. וַיִּ֫רֶב	j. she saw

Answers

1. e
2. d
3. g
4. j
5. c
6. h
7. b
8. a
9. i
10. f

Lesson 21

In This Lesson

1. Distinctive Qal Jussive Forms
   III-*Hē*
   II-*Wāw/Yōḏ*
2. The Qal Cohortative of Weak Verbs
3. The Qal Imperative: strong verb קְטֹל/קְטַל; weak roots
4. Imperative Forms with Final ָה -
5. Negative Commands
6. Imperatives as Interjections
   רְאֵה ("see!" "ah!"), קוּם ("come!"), הָבָה ("come!"), לְכָה ("come!")
7. The Imperative with a Redundant ל
8. Commands in Narrative Sequence
   impv. + ו-impv.: impv.
   impv. + ו-perf.: impv. force in perf. clause
   impv. + ו-impf./coh.: purpose/result clause ("so that. . .")
   juss. + ו-impv.: purpose/result clause ("so that. . ."), not command

Terms to Know

cohortative (XVIII)
imperative
interjection
jussive (XVIII)

Tips

1. The Qal imperative form looks like a "shortened" Qal imperfect (Qal imperfect minus preformative), making it an easy form to recognize.

2. Note the vowel under the first radical in Qal imperative forms. The first vowel is typically the same for ms-fp and fs-mp. This is true also for the vowel under the second radical for Qal imperatives of strong verbs, I-Guttural verbs, and II-Guttural verbs.

3. Do not be confused by the imperative forms with final ָה - (XXI.4, p. 241). They have the same meaning as imperatives without the final ָה -.

ANSWER KEY

21.a.

1. Qal *Wāw*-consecutive 3ms יָצַק to pour out
   This verb behaves like a I-*Nûn* verb (XVI.8.c, p. 185).

2. Qal impv. ms יָהַב w/ final ָה to give
   As in the imperfect, the first radical does not appear in the imperative for I-*Yōḏ* verbs (XXI.3.e, note i, p. 239). When the imperative form takes the final ָה-, the base is typically shortened, contracted, or reduced (XXI.4.a, p. 241). In this example, however, the base is lengthened and accented because it is in pause.

3. Qal impv. fs עָלָה to go up

4. Qal juss. 3ms שִׂים to set
   The jussives of II-*Wāw/Yōḏ* verbs differ from their corresponding imperfect forms and from the *Wāw*-consecutive forms (XXI.1.b, p. 235–36).

5. Qal juss. 3ms עָלָה to go up
   The jussives of III-*Hē* verbs are usually identical to the corresponding *Wāw*-consecutive forms without the conjunction (XXI.1.a, p. 235).

6. Qal impv. ms נָתַן w/final ָה to give

7. Qal impv. ms נָצַר to guard

8. Qal impv. mp יָהַב to give

9. Qal juss. 3ms עָשָׂה to make

10. Qal impv. ms עָלָה to go up

11. Qal *Wāw*-consecutive 2ms/3fs נוּחַ to rest

12. Qal juss. 3ms שִׁית to put

13. Qal juss. 2ms נָטָה to stretch out
    When the second-person imperfect form of III-*Hē* and II-*Wāw/Yōḏ* roots functions as a command (XVIII.4.c, p. 209; GKC §109a, p. 321), it may take the shortened jussive form, as it does here (see the third-person form for this root in XXI.1.a, p. 235; see also BDB, p. 639).

14. Qal impv. ms שִׁית w/ final ָה to put

15. Qal *Wāw*-consecutive 3ms שִׁית to put

16. Qal impv. mp שִׁיר to sing

17. Qal impv. ms זָכַר w/ final ָה to remember

18. Qal juss. 3ms קוּם to rise
19. Qal impv. ms שׁוּב w/ final הָ to return
20. Qal *Wāw*-consecutive 3mp יָצַק to pour out
This verb behaves like a I-*Nûn* verb (XVI.8.c, p. 185), with loss of gemination in a "Sqnmlwy" letter (VI.7, p. 59).
21. Qal *Wāw*-consecutive 1cs טָהֵר to be clean/pure

21.b.

1. שִׁיר
2. בְּנֵה
The Qal imperative ms ending for III-*Hē* verbs is always הֵ -, not הֶ -, as in the imperfect 2ms (XXI.3.d, note i, p. 238).
3. יָמֹת
The jussives of II-*Wāw/Yōḏ* verbs differ from their corresponding imperfect forms and from the *Wāw*-consecutive forms (XXI.1.b, p. 235–36).
4. מוּת
5. שְׁתֵה
The Qal imperative ms ending for III-*Hē* verbs is always הֵ -, not הֶ -, as in the imperfect 2ms (XXI.3.d, note i, p. 238).
6. עֲשׂוּ
7. תָּשֹׁב
8. רְאוּ
9. הֱיֵה
For the verbs הָיָה and חָיָה, the first syllable is *ḥāṭep̄-sěḡôl,* not *ḥāṭep̄-páṯaḥ* (XXI.3.d, note ii, pp. 238–39).
10. הֱיוּ
11. נְטֵה
12. יֵשֵׁב
13. שְׁבוּ
14. שׁוּבוּ
15. שְׁבִי
16. שֵׁבְנָה

17. לְכִי
The verb הָלַךְ behaves like a I-*Wāw* verb in the imperative, just as it does in the Qal imperfect (XXI.3.e, note ii, p. 239; cf. XIX.5.c, p. 218).

18. קַח
The verb לָקַח behaves like a I-*Nûn* verb (XXI.3.f, note ii, p. 240).

19. סְעוּ

20. תְּנוּ

21.c. 1 Kgs 3:4–15

v 4: לִזְבֹּחַ "to sacrifice"—יַעֲלֶה "(subject) offered."

v 5: נִרְאָה "(subject) appeared"—לָךְ instead of expected form לְךָ (pausal form, IX.2.a, note ii, p. 95); so also v 13.

v 7: צֵאת וָבֹא "to go out and to come in"; the vocalization of the conjunction as וָ occurs with certain pairs of words, and it may also occur when the conjunction is immediately before certain accented syllables, as in תֹהוּ וָבֹהוּ in Gen 1:2 (BDB, p. 251; Joüon, §104c, d, pp. 347–49).

v 8: לֹא־יִמָּנֶה וְלֹא יִסָּפֵר "cannot be numbered and cannot be counted"—מֵרֹב This is a special use of מִן (VII.5, pp. 73–74 and BDB מִן 6.d, p. 582).

v 9: לִשְׁפֹּט "to judge"—לְהָבִין "to discern"—טוֹב לְרָע The preposition לְ indicates a separation or distinction between the two concepts being considered (see also Num 30:17; Deut 17:8; 2 Sam 19:36; BDB, p. 516).

v 11: יַעַן אֲשֶׁר See X.8, pp. 111–12—הָבִין לִשְׁמֹעַ "discernment (lit. 'discerning') to hear."

v 12: וְנָבוֹן "and intelligent."

v 14: לִשְׁמֹר "to keep."

v 15: וַיַּעַל—וַיִּיקַץ = וַיִּקַץ "and he offered up."

Review the Concepts

Parse the verbs and translate the following phrases, paying close attention to the sense of the verbs in narrative sequence (XXI.8).

1. שִׁיר לָהּ וְתָנַח

2. שִׁיתָה יְהוָה מוֹרָה לָהֶם וְיֵדְעוּ גוֹיִם אֱנוֹשׁ הֵמָּה

3. אִסְפִּי הַבְּגָדִים וְכַבְּסִי אֹתָם

4. לֵךְ וְאַל־תִּכָּשֵׁל

Answers

1. שִׁיר Qal impv. ms; נוּחַ Qal impf. 3fs
   Sing to her so that she may rest.
   (imperative + ו-imperfect: purpose clause)

2. שִׁית Qal impv. ms w/ final ָה -; יָדַע Qal impf. 3ms
   O YHWH, put fear in them so that the nations may know that they are (only) human.
   (imperative + ו-imperfect: purpose clause; this may also be read as imperative + ו-jussive: "O YHWH, put fear in them, and let the nations know...")

3. אָסַף Qal impv. fs; כָּבַס Qal impv. fs
   Gather the clothes and wash them.
   (imperative + imperative)

4. הָלַךְ Qal impv. ms; כָּשַׁל Qal impf. 2ms
   Go, and may you not stumble.
   (imperative + negated imperfect)

Lesson 22

In This Lesson

1. The Imperfect and Imperative with Object Suffixes
   vowel changes in verb with addition of object suffix
   forms of the object suffixes
   occasional added *-en-* element
2. The Qal Infinitive Absolute: strong verb קָטוֹל; select weak roots
3. Uses of the Infinitive Absolute

Terms to Know

imperative (XXI)
imperfect (XVIII)
infinitive absolute
object suffix (XVII)
thematic vowel (XVIII)

Tips

1. The student may wish to review The Perfect with Object Suffixes (XVII). The idea here is the same: object suffixes are used in place of the independent object pronouns (learned in lesson IX, p. 99).

2. The object suffixes are essentially those of Type B in IX.2.b, p. 96, except for the 3mp and 3fp forms. Where these suffixes take a connecting vowel, however, they use an *i*-class connecting vowel (*ṣērê* or *sĕgōl*; see XXII.1.c, p. 248). Compare, for instance, יִשְׁמְרֵנִי "he will keep me" (impf.) to שְׁמָרַנִי "he has kept me" (perf.).

3. The Qal infinitive absolute is easily recognized, though the alert student will note that it is identical to a common adjective pattern (e.g., גָּדוֹל, קָטוֹן). The infinitive absolute takes an impressive range of meanings; see Review the Concepts below for practice translating this verb form.

Answer Key

22.a.

1. Qal inf. abs. נָתַן to give
2. Qal inf. abs. קָנָה to acquire

3. Qal impf. 3ms נָתַן + obj. sfx. 2ms to give
   Note shortening of *ṣērê* to *sĕgōl* (XXII.1.a.ii, p. 247).

4. Qal impv. ms נָתַן + obj. sfx. 3ms to give
   For this form, see XXII.1.b.iii, p. 248.

5. Qal impv. ms נָתַן + obj. sfx. 3mp to give

6. Qal perf. 3ms שָׁמַר + obj. sfx. 2ms to watch

7. Qal impv. ms שָׁמַר + obj. sfx. 1cs to guard
   The common *qĕṭōl* type of the Qal ms impv. becomes *qoṭl-* with object suffix (XXII.1.b.i, p. 247–48).

8. Qal impv. ms שָׁמַר + obj. sfx. 3ms to guard

9. Qal impf. 3ms בָּנָה + obj. sfx. 3ms to build

10. Qal impf. 3ms קָנָה + obj. sfx. 3ms to acquire

11. Qal impf. 1cs בָּנָה + obj. sfx. 3fs to build
    The additional *-en-* element is added unpredictably to impf. or impv. with object suffix (XXII.1.c, p. 249) but with no effect on meaning.

12. Qal impf. 3ms שִׂים + obj. sfx. 1cs to place, set

13. Qal impf. 2ms/3fs שָׁמַר + obj. sfx. 3mp to guard

14. Qal impv. ms שָׁמַע + obj. sfx. 1cs to hear

15. Qal impf. 3ms חָגַר + obj. sfx. 3fs to gird

22.b.

1. Prov 4:1–6

v 1: וְהַקְשִׁ֫יבוּ "and pay attention"—לָדַ֫עַת "to know"

v 4: וַיֹּ֫רֵנִי "he instructed me"—יִתְמָךְ The subject must be ms, and in fact it is לִבֶּ֫ךָ (word order: verb, direct object, subject)—וֶחְיֵה The *sĕgōl* under the conjunction is unexpected, perhaps reflecting original *וְחֱיֵה (Rule of *Šĕwāʾ;* VI.6.d, p. 58); in any case, word-initial ו will always be the conjunction (excepting the word וָו "peg" and some proper nouns; BDB, p. 255).

v 5: תֵּט See annotation to Lesson XXI, exercise a.13.

2. Amos 7:10–17

v 10: לְהָכִיל "to endure."

v 11: גָּלֹה יִגְלֶה For use of the infinitive absolute, see XXII.3.b, p. 250.

v 12: תִּנָּבֵא "you may prophesy."

v 13: לֹא־תוֹסִיף "you shall not continue"—לְהִנָּבֵא "to prophesy."

v 14: בֶן־נָבִיא In the Hebrew language, "son of" may indicate membership in a class, as in בֶּן־אָדָם "human being, member of humanity" (BDB בֵּן 7.a, p. 121); bear this in mind when translating this phrase.

v 15: וַיִּקָּחֵנִי Recall which strong root behaves, in the imperfect, as if it were I-*Nûn* (XIX.4.d, p. 217)—הִנָּבֵא "Prophesy!"

v 16: לֹא תִנָּבֵא "you shall not prophesy"—וְלֹא תַטִּיף "you shall not preach."

v 17: תְּחֻלָּק "shall be divided up."

22.c. 1 Kgs 3:16–28

v 16: שְׁתַּיִם "two."

v 17: הָאַחַת "the one" as attributive adjective modifying הָאִשָּׁה—בִּי אֲדֹנִי "Please, my lord!" (an introductory formula used to begin conversation with a male superior)—אֶחָד "one" as attributive adjective modifying בְּבַיִת.

v 18: הַשְּׁלִישִׁי "the third" as attributive adjective modifying בַּיּוֹם—לְלִדְתִּי "of my child-bearing"—זוּלָתִי "except"—שְׁתַּיִם "two of."

v 20: וַתַּשְׁכִּיבֵהוּ "and she laid him."

v 21: לְהֵינִיק "to nurse"—וָאֶתְבּוֹנֵן "I looked closely."

v 22: וַתְּדַבֵּרְנָה "and they spoke."

v 24: וַיָּבִאוּ "and they brought."

v 25: לִשְׁנָיִם "into two"—לְאַחַת ... לְאַחַת "to one ... to the other."

v 26: נִכְמְרוּ "(subject) were moved"—וְהָמֵת אַל־תְּמִיתֻהוּ "but please do not kill him."

v 27: וְהָמֵת לֹא תְמִיתֻהוּ "you shall not kill him."

v 28: וַיִּרְאוּ The *méṯeḡ* (Excursus B.3, p. 66) should help you determine this root (also XIX.6.b, note, p. 219)—לַעֲשׂוֹת "to do."

REVIEW THE CONCEPTS

There is in English no single construction corresponding to the Hebrew infinitive absolute. Further, the many uses of the infinitive absolute may take some getting used to. Again, the student may take comfort in the ease with which this form is recognized: קָטוֹל!

Translate these biblical phrases and try to determine which of the following best describes the usage of the infinitive absolute verb (XXII.3, pp. 250–52): (a) a verbal noun; (b) adding certainty to a finite verb of the same root; (c) intensifying a preceding imperative; (d) action simultaneous with another infinitive absolute (perhaps, as הָלוֹךְ, indicating continuance); (e) functioning as an imperative; or (f) action concurrent with a finite verb.

1. בְּכוּ בָכוֹ לַהֹלֵךְ (Jer 22:10)
2. נָשֹׂא אֶת־רֹאשׁ בְּנֵי קְהָת (Num 4:2)
3. וַיֵּלֶךְ דָּוִד הָלוֹךְ וְגָדוֹל (2 Sam 5:10)
4. וְזֶה־לְּךָ הָאוֹת אָכוֹל הַשָּׁנָה סָפִיחַ (2 Kgs 19:29)
5. וְעָלוּ עָלֹה וּבָכֹה (2 Sam 15:30)
6. וַיֹּאמְרוּ הָאֶחָד בָּא־לָגוּר וַיִּשְׁפֹּט שָׁפוֹט (Gen 19:9)
7. וַתָּקָם חַנָּה אַחֲרֵי אָכְלָה בְשִׁלֹה וְאַחֲרֵי שָׁתֹה (1 Sam 1:9)
8. וַתַּעַן לָהֶם מִרְיָם שִׁירוּ לַיהוָה כִּי־גָאֹה גָּאָה (Exod 15:21)
9. וַיִּתְקְעוּ בַּשּׁוֹפָרוֹת וְנָפוֹץ הַכַּדִּים אֲשֶׁר בְּיָדָם (Judg 7:19)
10. וְנָתוֹן הַלְּבוּשׁ וְהַסּוּס עַל־יַד־אִישׁ מִשָּׂרֵי הַמֶּלֶךְ (Esth 6:9)

Answers

1. Weep for the one who is going! (c)
2. Count (lit. "take the head") of the Kohathites! (see BDB **נָשָׂא** Qal 3.d, p. 671) (e)
3. David went on and continually became greater. (d)
4. This shall be to you the sign: eating, this year, what is wild. (a: the "eating" is "the sign")
5. They went up, weeping. (d)
6. They said, "This one has come as an alien yet indeed would judge! (b)
7. Hannah arose after she ate in Shiloh, and after she drank. (f: her drinking is concurrent with her eating)
8. Miriam answered them: "Sing to YHWH, for he has triumphed indeed!" (b)
9. They blew the trumpets while smashing the jars that were in their hands. (f)
10. Give the clothing and the horse to a man from among the king's nobles. (e)

Lesson 23

In This Lesson

1. The Qal Infinitive Construct
   strong verb קְטֹל
   with suffixed pronouns
      usually -קָטְל
      -קְטָל with 2ms and 2mp suffixes
2. The Qal Infinitive Construct of Weak Verbs
3. Uses of the Infinitive Construct
   verbal noun
   to express intention (used after לְ)
   to elaborate and clarify (used after לְ)
   to indicate incipient action (used after לְ)
   used with בְּ or כְּ in temporal clauses
4. The Negation of Infinitives
   most commonly negated by לְבִלְתִּי (not)
   may be negated by בְּלֹא (without) or מִבְּלִי/בְּלִי (without)
5. Synopsis of Verbs in Qal
   See the chart on page 260.

Terms to Know

prefixed prepositions (VI)
suffixed pronouns (IX)
verbal noun

Tips

1. Like the infinitive absolute, the infinitive construct is not inflected for gender, number, or person, but unlike the absolute, it may take a suffixed pronoun.

2. The suffixed pronoun may be the subject or the object of the infinitive construct; one can only determine which it is from context (XXIII.1.c, pp. 255–56).

3. This lesson introduces the last Qal verbal form! Take special note of the Synopsis of Verbs in Qal on page 260.

ANSWER KEYS

23.a.

1. שְׁמֹר
2. שְׁמֹעַ
3. זְכֹר
4. קַ֫חַת
   The verb לָקַח, like some I-*Nûn* verbs, behaves in the infinitive construct like I-*Wāw* verbs, losing the initial radical (XXIII.2.d.ii, p. 257).
5. צֵאת
   Infinitive constructs of I-*Wāw* verbs do not retain the initial radical, and they take an anomalous ת- ending (XXIII.2.c, p. 256). In this II-*ʾĀlep̄* root, the א quiesces and the preceding vowel lengthens (XXIII.2.c, note ii, p. 257).
6. לֶ֫דֶת
7. רֶ֫שֶׁת
8. נְתֹן/תֵּת
   There are two types of infinitive constructs for I-*Nûn* verbs (XXIII.2.d, p. 257).
9. דַּ֫עַת
10. בְּחֹר
11. עֲמֹד
12. נְפֹל
13. בְּנוֹת
    Infinitive constructs of III-*Hē* verbs always end with וֹת- (XXIII.2.b, p. 256).
14. גְּלוֹת
15. עֲשׂוֹת
16. הֲלֹךְ/לֶ֫כֶת
    This verb behaves like a I-*Wāw* verb (XXIII.2.c, note i, p. 257).
17. שֶׁ֫בֶת
18. חֲזֹק
19. רֶ֫דֶת

20. אֱכֹל
Note that I-*ʾÁlep̄* verbs have *ḥấṭep̄-sĕḡōl* instead of *ḥấṭep̄-páṯaḥ* in the first syllable (XXIII.2.a, p. 256).

21. שָׁמְרוּ

22. תִּתִּי
With the strong *dāḡēš* in the second ת, there is no need for compensatory lengthening with the preformative (XXIII.2.d.ii, note ii, p. 258).

23. תִּתּוֹ

24. לֶכְתּוֹ
See XXIII.2.c, note i, p. 257.

25. שִׁבְתִּי
See XXIII.2.c, p. 256.

26. רִשְׁתּוֹ

27. בּוֹאֲךָ

28. מָצְאֲךָ

29. אֲכָלְךָ

30. קַחְתִּי
See XXIII.2.d.ii, p. 257.

23.b. Eccl 3:1–9

v 1: To review the translation of כֹּל, see XI.5.b, p. 123—עֵת Review V.1.b, note ii, p. 39, regarding identify the root.

v 5: לְהַשְׁלִיךְ "for casting" (also in v 6)—מֵחַבֵּק "for embracing."

v 6: לְבַקֵּשׁ "for seeking"—לְאַבֵּד "for destroying."

v 7: לְדַבֵּר "for speaking."

23.c. Josh 1:1–9

Study tip: Like nouns, phrases can be in apposition, clarifying or elaborating a preceding word or phrase (VII.7, p. 74). Look for the use of appositional phrases in this passage.

v 4: For translation of מְבוֹא הַשָּׁמֶשׁ, see BDB מָבוֹא 2, pp. 99–100. Note the disrupted word order in this verse (XIII.4.b, pp. 150–51).

v 5: לֹא־יִתְיַצֵּב אִישׁ "no one shall stand" (lit.: "a man shall not stand")—עִמָּךְ is a pausal form (also in v 9; IX.2.a, note ii, p. 95; Excursus B.5, p. 67)—לֹא אַרְפְּךָ "I will not fail you."

v 6: תַּנְחִיל "you will cause (object) to inherit (object)"—נִשְׁבַּעְתִּי "I swore."

v 7: תַּשְׂכִּיל "you will have success" (also in v 8).

v 8: תַּצְלִיחַ "you will make (object) prosper."

v 9: וְאַל־תֵּחָת "do not be dismayed."

23.d. Gen 3:1–14

v 1: On the translation of מִכֹּל here and in v 14, see VII.5, p. 73; XI.6.d, p. 124. There are several occurrences of the Qal imperfect and the *wayyiqṭōl* of אָכַל in this passage. For the forms, review XIX.1.d, notes ii–iii, p. 215; XX.4.a, p. 228.

v 4: On the use of מוֹת here, see XXII.3.b, p. 250.

v 5: For the form מִמֶּנּוּ, see IX.2.b, p. 96—וְנִפְקְחוּ "and (subject) will open"—טוֹב וָרָע The vocalization of the conjunction וָ occurs with certain pairs of words as well as when the conjunction is immediately before certain accented syllables, such as תֹהוּ וָבֹהוּ in Gen 1:2 (BDB, p. 251; Joüon, §104c, d, pp. 347–49).

v 6: וְנֶחְמָד "and desirable"—לְהַשְׂכִּיל "to make wise/successful."

v 7: וַתִּפָּקַחְנָה "and (subject) opened"—שְׁנֵיהֶם "two of them."

v 8: מִתְהַלֵּךְ "walking about"—For the translation of לְרוּחַ, see BDB לְ 6.a, p. 516—וַיִּתְחַבֵּא "(subject) hid himself."

v 9: On אַיֶּכָּה, see X.6.f, p. 111.

v 10: וָאֵחָבֵא "and I hid myself."

v 12: The *wayyiqṭōl* 1cs form of אָכַל is attested as וָאֹכַל and as the pausal form וָאֹכֵל here and in v 13 (BDB, p. 37; Excursus B.5, p. 67).

Review the Concepts

Match the verbal forms on pages 107–8 with the correct verbal patterns (one form will be used twice).

1. Qal impv.	a. קֹטֵל
2. Qal perf.	b. קִטֵּל
3. Qal pass. ptc.	c. קְטֹל
4. Qal inf. abs.	d. קָטוּל
5. Qal act. ptc.	e. וַיִּקְטֹל

6. Qal impf.	f. הִקְטִיל
7. Piel perf.	g. קָטוֹל
8. Qal inf. cs.	h. קָטַל
9. Hiphil perf.	i. יִקְטֹל
10. Qal *Wāw*-consecutive	

Answers

1. c
2. h
3. d
4. g
5. a
6. i
7. b
8. c
9. f
10. e

Lesson 24

In This Lesson

1. The Piel Imperfect: strong verb יְקַטֵּל; weak forms
2. The Piel Jussive, *Wāw*-Consecutive, and Cohortative
   predictable forms except for III-*Hē* verb (lacks final ה)
   cohortative: אֲקַטְּלָה
3. The Piel Imperative: strong verb קַטֵּל; weak verb
   form: "shortened" Piel imperfect
4. The Piel Infinitives
   infinitive construct and infinitive absolute: קַטֵּל
5. Synopsis of Verbs in Piel: see the chart on page 267.
6. The Numerals
   cardinal numbers (see charts for forms, pp. 268–70)
   1: attributive (after noun)
   2: substantive (precedes noun)
   3–10: substantive, no agreement in gender or number
   11 and higher
   ordinal numbers (see chart for forms, p. 271)
   1st–10th: attributive
   11th and higher: attributive, uses cardinal numbers
7. Expressions of the Distributive
   repeating substantives ("two by two")
   preposition לְ ("every...")
   אִישׁ ("each")

Terms to Know

apposition (VII)
attributive (VII)
cardinal number
distributive
ordinal number
substantive (VII)

Tips

1. The Piel imperfect is easily identified by these three key characteristics (יְקַטֵּל):

(a) *šĕwāʾ* under the preformative
(b) *a*-vowel under the first radical
(c) doubling of the second radical

Even III-*Hē* verbs that do not have a doubled second radical (due to the loss of the final *Hē*) still have a *šĕwāʾ* in the prefix and an *a*-vowel under the first radical.

2. Like other imperative forms, the Piel imperative looks like a "shortened" Piel imperfect (Piel imperfect minus the prefix). It too has the standard characteristics of Piel: *a*-vowel under the first radical and doubling of the second radical.

Answer Key

24.a.

1. יְבַקַּע
   Gutturals prefer *a*-class vowels, so the Piel impf. forms tend to have the *yĕqaṭṭal* pattern instead of *yĕqaṭṭēl* (XXIV.1.d, p. 265).
2. תְּבַקְּשִׁי
3. בַּקֵּשׁ
4. בַּקֵּשׁ
5. אֲבַקְשָׁה
6. מָאֵן
   This verb has the expected compensatory lengthening required since the א does not take the *dāḡēš* (XXIV.1.b, p. 264).
7. יְמָאֲנוּ
8. יְמָהֲרוּ
9. מָהֵר
10. מַהֲרִי
11. מַהֵר
12. תְּמַהֵ֫רְנָה
13. יְבָרֵךְ
14. אֲבָרֵךְ
15. בָּרֵךְ
16. בָּרֲכִי
17. בָּרֲכוּ

18. יְכַסֶּה
19. אֲכַסֶּה
20. כַּסּוֹת
21. כַּלּוֹ
22. צַוֵּה
23. צַוּוֹת
24. יְצַו

The III-*Hē* verbs lack the expected *dāgēš* in the Piel jussive form (see XXIV.2.a, p. 265) and yet still have the expected *šěwāʾ* under the preformative and *a*-vowel under the first radical.

25. יַסֵּר
26. יְנַשֵּׁק
27. נַשְּׁקוּ
28. מְיַלֶּ֫דֶת
29. יְגַלֶּה
30. גַּלִּי

24.b. Deut 5:1–33

v 3: כִּי "but" after a negative; כִּי may be adversative.

v 5: לְהַגִּיד "to tell."

v 8: כָּל Remember that the translation depends on the definiteness of the noun that כֹּל qualifies (XI.5.b, p. 123).

v 9: לֹא־תִשְׁתַּחֲוֶה "you shall not bow down"—וְלֹא תָעָבְדֵם "and you shall not be made to serve them."

v 15: וַיֹּצִאֲךָ "but (subject) brought you out."

v 16: יַאֲרִיכֻן "(subject) may be prolonged."

v 21: וְלֹא תִתְאַוֶּה "you shall not covet."

v 22: קוֹל גָּדוֹל There is no preposition here, but it is clear that YHWH speaks with a great voice. The phrase is an adverbial accusative (see *IBHS,* 10.2.2, pp. 169–73).

v 27: וְאַתְּ (read וְאַתָּה)

v 29: מִי־יִתֵּן "would that" (or "if only…"; a common idiom)

v 30: לָכֶם The לְ has a reflexive sense, i.e., "turn yourselves." This may be called an "ethical dative" or "ingressive" use of the לְ (see *IBHS*, 11.2.10d, pp. 206–9).

REVIEW THE CONCEPTS

1. Put the following Hebrew numbers in order, from least to greatest.

a. שְׁמֹנֶה	f. מֵאָה	k. שְׁלֹשִׁים
b. אַלְפַּ֫יִם	g. חָמֵשׁ	l. אַרְבַּע
c. שֶׁ֫בַע	h. עֶ֫שֶׂר	m. שִׁשִּׁים
d. שָׁלֹשׁ	i. אֶ֫לֶף	n. מָאתַ֫יִם
e. שְׁנַ֫יִם	j. תִּשְׁעִים	

Write the following phrases in Hebrew

2. a third sign
3. four kings
4. one assembly
5. two idols
6. seven bulls
7. the tenth female slave
8. five hills

Answers

1. e, d, l, g, c, a, h, k, m, j, f, n, i, b
2. מוֹפֵת שְׁלִישִׁי
3. אַרְבָּעָה מְלָכִים
4. קָהָל אֶחָד
5. שְׁנֵי פְּסִילִים
6. שִׁבְעָה שְׁוָרִים or שִׁבְעַה שְׁוָרִים
7. הָאָמָה הָעֲשִׂירִית
8. חָמֵשׁ גְּבָעוֹת or חֲמֵשׁ גְּבָעוֹת

Lesson 25

In This Lesson

1. The Hiphil Imperfect: strong verb יַקְטִיל; select weak roots
2. The Hiphil Jussive, *Wāw*-Consecutive, and Cohortative
   jussive יַקְטֵל
   cohortative אַקְטִ֫ילָה
3. The Hiphil Imperative
   strong verb הַקְטֵל
4. The Hiphil Infinitives
   infinitive absolute = imperative
   infinitive construct הַקְטִיל
5. Synopsis of Verbs in Hiphil
   See the chart on page 283.
6. Translation of ו

Terms to Know

conjunctive/disjunctive (cf. XIII.4.b, p. 150)
jussive (XVIII, XXI)
preformative (XVIII)
thematic vowel (XVIII)

Tips

1. This lesson may be compared to XXIV, on the Piel imperfect; again, the student will combine two already-familiar concepts: the imperfect inflections and the Hiphil stem.

2. Just as the Piel imperfect is reminiscent of the Piel participle (both have vocal *šĕwāʾ* under the initial consonant; compare יְקַטֵּל with מְקַטֵּל), so is the Hiphil imperfect reminiscent of the Hiphil participle in the strong verb, taking a *pátaḥ* under the initial consonant (compare יַקְטִיל with מַקְטִיל). The Hiphil imperative and the infinitives share also this important identifying feature.

3. Recall that the preformative of the Qal imperfect of I-Guttural roots also takes an *a*-class vowel (XIX.1.d, p. 214), causing potential confusion with the Hiphil imperfect. The theme vowel will distinguish the two forms, except in many I-Guttural verbs that are also III-*Hē* (XXV.1.b, note, p. 276; XXV.1.e, note, pp. 277–78).

4. The basic Hebrew contractions (**-ay-* > *-ê-* and **-aw-* > *-ô-*) are once again helpful for one's understanding of the Hiphil imperfects of I-*Yōḏ* and I-*Wāw* roots, respectively (e.g., יֵטִיב < **yayṭîḇ*, יוֹשִׁיב < **yawšîḇ*, XXV.1.f–g, p. 278).

5. The student might want to review the characteristic shortening of certain jussive forms (XXI.1, pp. 235–36). In the Hiphil, this shortening of jussive verbs is usually simply from imperfect יַקְטִיל > jussive יַקְטֵל. III-*Hē* and I-*Nûn*/III-*Hē* roots pose particular challenges: see annotations to the exercises for detailed help with these forms.

ANSWER KEY

25.a.

1. יַשְׁמִיעוּ
2. הַשְׁמִ֫יעוּ
3. תַּעֲמֵ֫דְנָה
4. תַּעֲמֹ֫דְנָה

   Compare the different thematic vowels in nos. 3 and 4 (XIX.1.d, p. 214; XXV.1.b, pp. 275–76).
5. יַעֲלֶה
6. יַעֲלֶה

   Except for 1cs forms, the Qal and Hiphil imperfects of I-Guttural/III-*Hē* roots will be identical (XXV.1.e, note, p. 277).
7. הַעֲלֵי
8. אַעֲלֶה
9. אֶעֱלֶה

   See annotation to no. 6 above.
10. אוֹשִׁיב

    This form derives from **ʾawšîḇ* (XXV.1.f, p. 278; see also tip 4 above). Compare with no. 27 below.
11. אָשִׁיב
12. אָשׁוּב
13. הָשֵׁב
14. הַעֲלוֹת
15. הַעֲלֵה
16. יַכֶּה

17. אַכֶּה

18. יַךְ
The imperfect is יַכֶּה; shortened jussive form *yakk > yak̲ (XXV.2.a.iii, note γ, p. 281).

19. נַגִּיד

20. הַגֵּד

21. הַגֵּד

22. תְּבִאֶינָה

23. תְּבוֹאֶינָה

24. יֶגֶל
The imperfect is יִגְלֶה; shortened jussive form *yagl > *yáḡel > yéḡel. Compare with *a*-class segolate nouns, such as *malk > *málek̲ > mélek̲ (XXV.2.a.iii, note α, p. 280).

25. יַעַל

26. יַעַל
XXI.1.a., p. 235.

27. הֵיטִיב
This form derives from *hayṭîḇ (XXV.1.e, p. 278; see also tip 4 above). Compare with no. 10 above.

28. הֵיטִ֫יבִי

29. הַרְבֵּה

30. הַרְבּוֹת

25.b. Ps 1

v 1: אַשְׁרֵי This apparently construct noun functions independently as a nominal exclamation (*IBHS,* 40.2.3b, p. 681)—עֲצַת hint: I-*Yōḏ* root.

v 3: עָלֵ֫הוּ This suffixed noun derives from the frequent verbal root עָלָה "to ascend," but the noun itself is rare—תִּדְּפֶ֫נּוּ Remember the fairly common "resumptive object suffix" (XVII.4, p. 201).

25.c. Ps 23

v 2: נְאוֹת BDB will sometimes help one to find a root—יְנַהֲלֵ֫נִי To help determine the stem, note the vocal *šĕwāʾ* under the preformative (XXIV.1.a, note i, p. 264); remember also virtual doubling (IV.2.a.i.β, p. 26).

v 3: יְשׁוֹבֵב "he restores."

v 4: גֵיא צַלְמָוֶת Again, remember that BDB will sometimes help one to locate a root—יְנַחֲמֻנִי See annotation above to v 2.

25.d. Ps 148

v 3: כּוֹכְבֵי אוֹר To help understand the NRSV translation, see XI.4, p. 122.

v 4: שְׁמֵי הַשָּׁמָיִם See XI.6.c, p. 124.

v 5: וְנִבְרָאוּ "and they were created."

v 6: יַעֲבוֹר impersonal use of 3ms (XIV.7.a, p. 166).

v 13: נִשְׂגָּב "exalted."

v 14: וַיָּרֶם To determine the root, see XX.4.c, p. 228.

REVIEW THE CONCEPTS

Hiphil jussive challenge! The weak roots with this form take some additional practice. The following short biblical phrases each contain a Hiphil jussive form of a weak root. Translate each phrase.

1. וְיַגֶּד־לָנוּ יְהוָה אֱלֹהֶיךָ אֶת־הַדֶּרֶךְ (Jer 42:3)
2. יָקֵם יְהוָה אֶת־דְּבָרֶיךָ (Jer 28:6)
3. יַפְתְּ אֱלֹהִים לְיֶפֶת (Gen 9:27)
4. וְיָסֵר הַצְפַרְדְּעִים מִמֶּנִּי וּמֵעַמִּי (Exod 8:4)
5. יֹסֵף יְהוָה לִי בֵּן אַחֵר (Gen 30:24)
6. וְיַגֶּד־לָנוּ אֶת־הַחִידָה (Judg 14:15)
7. יֵיטֵב אֱלֹהֶיךָ אֶת־שֵׁם שְׁלֹמֹה (1 Kgs 1:47)
8. אַל־יָנַע עַצְמֹתָיו (2 Kgs 23:18)

Answers

1. May YHWH your God show us the way (I-*Nûn*).
2. May YHWH establish your words (II-*Wāw*).
3. May God open (a space) to Japheth (III-*Hē*).
4. And may he take the frogs from me and from my people (II-*Wāw*).
5. May YHWH add to me another son (I-*Wāw*).
(Observe that the I-*Wāw* Hiphil jussive can be identical to the Qal active participle of the same root!)

6. May he reveal to us the riddle (I-*Nûn*).
7. May your God make esteemed the name of Solomon (I-*Yôḏ*).
8. May no one shake his bones (II-*Wāw*/III-Guttural).

Lesson 26

In This Lesson

1. The Niphal Pattern
2. The Meaning of Verbs in Niphal
   reflexive, tolerative; reciprocal; passive; resultative; middle
3. The Niphal Perfect
   strong verb נִקְטַל
   weak verbs
4. The Niphal Imperfect
   strong verb יִקָּטֵל
   weak verbs
5. The Niphal Imperative: strong verb הִקָּטֵל
6. The Niphal Infinitives
   infinitive absolute נִקְטֹל and הִקָּטֹל
   infinitive construct (same as impv.) הִקָּטֵל
7. The Niphal Participle: strong verb נִקְטָל
8. Synopsis of Verbs in Niphal

Terms to Know

assimilated נ (IV)
infixed
middle
passive (VIII)
reciprocal
reflexive; tolerative
resultative

Tips

1. The Niphal perfect is marked by a prefixed נ and the perfect afformatives.

2. The Niphal imperfect strong verb is marked by the "Niphal triangle": *ḥîreq* as the vowel of the preformative (except 1cs), assimilated נ in the first radical, and the vowel *qāmeṣ* under the first radical.

3. The Niphal imperative is marked by a -הִ prefix and an assimilated נ in the first radical. The Niphal imperative strong verb can be distinguished from any Hiphil form by the "Niphal triangle."

4. The Niphal infinitive construct is identical to the Niphal ms imperative (compare XXVI.5 and 6b, pp. 293–94).

5. The Niphal ms participle is similar to the Niphal perfect, but the participle has a *qā́meṣ* in the second syllable, while the perfect has a *páṭaḥ*.

Answer Key

26.a.

1. נִשְׁמַע
2. נִשְׁמָע
3. נֶאֶסְפָּה
4. נֶאֶסְפּוּ
5. הֵעָזֵב

   Compensatory lengthening occurs in the prefix vowel with I-Guttural verbs (see synopsis on p. 295); this also occurs in the Niphal imperfect (XXVI.4.b, p. 292).
6. הֵאָסְפִי
7. נָכוֹן
8. נָכוֹן
9. נָפוֹצָה
10. נָפוֹצֶת
11. יִפּוֹצוּ
12. אִפּוֹץ
13. נְפוֹצוֹתֶם
14. יִלָּחֲמוּ
15. נִלְחַמְתִּי
16. נִשְׁבַּעְתִּי
17. הִשָּׁבְעוּ
18. נִמְנָה
19. הִמָּנוֹת

    For this form of the III-*Hē* infinitive construct, see XXVI.6, p. 294; XXIII.2.b, p. 256.
20. נִמָּנֶה

21. נִבֵּיתָ/נִבֵּאתָ
The quiescent א is sometimes omitted (XIV.2, note, p. 161).

22. הִנָּבֵא
The ms participle of II-*Wāw/Yōḏ* verbs is identical to the perfect 3ms (XXVI.7.a, pp. 294–95).

23. הִנָּבֵא

24. נִנָּבֵא

25. נוֹדְעָה
Original **aw* contracts to *ô* (XXVI.3.c, p. 291).

26. נוֹדָע

27. הִוָּדַע

28. נִטָּעוּ

26.b. Gen 32:1–33

v 1: The Piel *wayyiqṭōl* 3ms form of בָּרַךְ typically takes a *sĕḡōl* after the ר.

v 3: For רָאָם, review III-*Hē* perfect verbs with suffixes (XVII.2.b, p. 200).

v 5: וָאֵחַר < *וָאֶאֱחַר (see XIX.1.d, note iii, p. 215).

v 8: וַיֵּצֶר לוֹ "and he became anxious."

v 9: וְהִכָּהוּ For the basic verbal form, see XVI.7, pp. 184–85; for the form with the suffixed pronoun, see XVII.2.b, p. 200.

v 10: For the translation of שׁוּב ... וְאֵיטִיבָה, see XXI.8.c, p. 243; XXV.6.b.i, p. 285.

v 11: For לְ + הָיָה, see BDB הָיָה 2.e, p. 226.

v 18: On the translation of כִּי here, review the possibilities in X Vocabulary, p. 113.

v 19: For the translation of וְ as "then," see XXV.6.b.i, p. 285.

Review the Concepts

Translate the following and identify the use of the Niphal verb (XXVI.2, pp. 288–89).

1. בַּיּוֹם הַזֶּה נִבְקְעוּ כָּל־מַעְיְנֹת תְּהוֹם רַבָּה (Gen 7:11)
2. שֹׁפֵךְ דַּם הָאָדָם בָּאָדָם דָּמוֹ יִשָּׁפֵךְ (Gen 9:6)
3. וַיֶּעְתַּר יִצְחָק לַיהוָה ... וַיֵּעָתֶר לוֹ יְהוָה (Gen 25:21)

4. וּבְנֵי יִשְׂרָאֵל אָכְלוּ אֶת־הַמָּן אַרְבָּעִים שָׁנָה עַד־בֹּאָם אֶל־אֶרֶץ נוֹשָׁבֶת (Exod 16:35)

5. וְכִי־יִנָּצוּ אֲנָשִׁים וְנָגְפוּ אִשָּׁה הָרָה (Exod 21:22)

Answers

1. On that day all the springs of the great deep burst open.
   Niphal of בָּקַע—middle

2. One who sheds the blood of a human, by a human shall his blood be shed.
   Niphal of שָׁפַךְ—passive (The definite forms of אָדָם should be translated generically.)

3. Isaac prayed to YHWH, and YHWH let himself be entreated by him.
   Niphal of עָתַר—tolerative

4. The Israelites ate manna forty years, until they came to a habitable land.
   Niphal of יָשַׁב—resultative, functioning as an adjective (XXVI.2.d, p. 289)

5. When men are fighting one another and strike a pregnant woman
   Niphal of נָצָה—reciprocal

Lesson 27

In This Lesson

1. The Hithpael Pattern
   key characteristics: infixed תּ, doubling of second radical
2. The Meaning of Hithpael Verbs
   reflexive, reciprocal, iterative, estimative
3. The Hithpael of the Strong Verb: perfect הִתְקַטֵּל; imperfect יִתְקַטֵּל
4. The Metathesis and Assimilation of the Infixed *Tāw*
   metathesis with sibilants (ס, צ, שׂ, שׁ)
   assimilation with dentals (ד, ט, ת) or other radicals (i.e., נ, כ)
5. The Hithpael of Weak Verbs
6. Synopsis of Verbs in Hithpael (see chart, p. 302)
7. The Hishtaphel Pattern
   used with the root חוה
   perfect הִשְׁתַּחֲוָה
   imperfect יִשְׁתַּחֲוֶה
8. Oaths
   positive statement: כִּי, כִּי אִם, or אִם לֹא
   negative statement: אִם

Terms to Know

dental
estimative
iterative
reciprocal (XXVI)
reflexive (XXVI)
sibilant (VI)

Tips

1. The Hithpael and Hishtaphel patterns are not difficult to recognize because of their distinctive preformatives (הִתְ-/יִתְ-, etc.). The Hishtaphel is all the more distinctive since it is attested with only one Hebrew root: חוה ("to bow down, worship").

2. Oath expressions may at first seem tricky: a positive oath can contain the particle לֹא, but a negative oath does not have לֹא. Think of

elliptical threats such as "If you do not turn off that TV..." (= "Turn off that TV") or "If you spill that milk..." (= "Do not spill that milk").

ANSWER KEY

27.a.

1. הִתְמַכֵּר
2. יִתְמַכְּרוּ
3. אֶשְׁתַּמֵּר
   Here the infixed ת shows metathesis with שׁ, a sibilant (XXVII.4.a, p. 300).
4. הִתְבַּקְּעוּ
5. הִתְגַּדַּ֫לְתִּי
6. מִתְדַּבֵּר
7. הִתְוַדָּה
8. הִטָּהֲרוּ
   The *dāgēš* in the ט indicates that the infixed ת has assimilated into the ט, a dental (XXVII.4.b, p. 301). Since the ה cannot take the strong *dāgēš*, as we would expect in the second radical of the Hithpael, the vowel preceding it is compensatorily lengthened (XXVII.5.a, p. 301 and XV.3.a.i, p. 175).
9. יִטָּהֲרוּ
10. מִטַּהֵר
11. הִטָּהֲרוּ
12. מִתְוַדִּים
13. אֶתְוַדַּע
   The first radical of this original I-*Wāw* verb is retained since it is preceded by -אֶתְ (XXVII.5.b, p. 301; cf. IV.2.c.ii, p. 28).
14. נִצְטַדֵּק
   Here the infixed ת shows metathesis with צ, a sibilant, and the ת has changed to a ט (XXVII.4.a, p. 300).
15. תִּשְׁתַּפֵּךְ
   Here the infixed ת shows metathesis with שׁ, a sibilant (XXVII.4.a, p. 300).
16. הִתְגַּלּוֹת

17. יִתְבָּרֵךְ
Since the ר cannot take the strong *dāgēš*, as we would expect in the second radical of the Hithpael, the vowel preceding it is compensatorily lengthened (XXVII.5.a, p. 301 and XV.3.a.i, p. 175).

18. מִתְבָּרֵךְ

19. הִשְׁתַּחֲוָה

20. יִשְׁתַּחֲוֶה

21. יִתְגַּל

22. הִשְׁתַּחֲוֶה
This form is conjectural and unattested in the Hebrew Bible.

27.b. 1 Sam 3

v 2: הֵחֵלּוּ "began."

v 9: אִם ... וְ "if" ... then."

v 11: תְּצִלֶּינָה "(subject) will tingle."

v 12: הָחֵל "the beginning."

REVIEW THE CONCEPTS

Learn to swear in Hebrew! Translate the following oaths and references to oaths into English:

1. וַיִּשָּׁבַע שָׁאוּל חַי־יְהוָה אִם־יוּמָת (1 Sam 19:6)
2. חַי אָנִי אִם־לֹא אָלָתִי אֲשֶׁר בָּזָה ... וּנְתַתִּיו בְּרֹאשׁוֹ (Ezek 17:19)
3. נִשְׁבַּעְתִּי בִּשְׁמִי הַגָּדוֹל אָמַר יְהוָה אִם־יִהְיֶה עוֹד שְׁמִי נִקְרָא בְּפִי כָּל־אִישׁ יְהוּדָה (Jer 44:26)
4. חַי־יְהוָה כִּי בֶן־מָוֶת הָאִישׁ הָעֹשֶׂה זֹאת (2 Sam 12:5)
5. וְעַתָּה הִשָּׁבְעָה לִּי בֵאלֹהִים ... אִם־תִּשְׁקֹר לִי (Gen 21:23)
6. וַיַּשְׁבִּעֵנִי אֲדֹנִי לֵאמֹר ... אִם־לֹא אֶל־בֵּית־אָבִי תֵּלֵךְ ... וְלָקַחְתָּ אִשָּׁה לִבְנִי (Gen 24:37–38)
7. וְעַתָּה הִשָּׁבְעָה לִּי בַּיהוָה אִם־תַּכְרִית אֶת־זַרְעִי אַחֲרָי (1 Sam 24:22)
8. יִשָּׁבַע־לִי ... הַמֶּלֶךְ שְׁלֹמֹה אִם־יָמִית אֶת־עַבְדּוֹ בֶּחָרֶב (1 Kgs 1:51)

Answers

1. Saul swore, "As YHWH lives: He shall not die!"

2. As I live: I will put on his head my oath that he despised.
3. "I swear by my great name," says YHWH, "my name shall no longer be invoked in the mouth of every person of Judah."
4. As YHWH lives: The man who did this is a dead man.
5. Now swear to me by God that you will not deal falsely with me.
6. My master made me swear, saying, "... you shall go to my father's house and get a wife for my son."
7. Now swear to me by YHWH that you will not cut off my descendants after me.
8. Let King Solomon swear to me not to kill his servant by the sword.

Lesson 28

In This Lesson

1. Geminate Verbs in Qal
   perfect סָבַב, תַּם
   imperfect יָסֹב, יֵתַם
2. Geminate Verbs in Niphal
   perfect נָסַב
   imperfect יִסַּב
3. Geminate Verbs in Hiphil
   perfect הֵסֵב
   imperfect יָסֵב
4. Geminate Roots and Other Roots

Terms to Know

dynamic/stative verbs (XIII, XVIII)
geminate (V)

Tips

1. It is worth remembering that geminate verbs are rather rare. Once one is familiar with the more common geminate verbal roots (see Vocabulary, p. 318), these will present only occasional trouble.

2. Although some geminate verbs may "masquerade" as other roots (see XXVIII.1.b, pp. 309–10; also XXVIII.4, pp. 316–17), the procedure is predictable: one might first look up the incorrect root, then upon reflection consider a possible geminate root. See Review the Concepts below for practice with these "masquerading" geminate forms.

3. By now the student is accustomed to this chapter's main challenge: assimilating a small amount of new knowledge with a great deal of review (Niphal and Hiphil stems, the *Wāw*-consecutive, behavior of "weak" roots, etc.). When doing the exercises, make careful use of the knowledge gained from earlier chapters, trying to complete your understanding of each unfamiliar form before continuing.

Answer Key

28.a

1. סַבּוֹתֶם
This additional וֹ element before the suffix was previously encountered with the Hiphil perfect of II-*Wāw/ Yôḏ* roots (XVI.10, note ii, p. 187). Here also in the Qal perfect of the strong geminate verb, it may be omitted, *סַבְתֶּם or *סַבְתֶם (XXVIII.1.a, note ii, p. 309).

2. יָסֹבּוּ

3. קַלּוֹתִי

4. קַלּוּ

5. הֲסִבּוֹתָ

6. יֵקַלּוּ

7. תַּם
Do not overlook these Type B Qal geminate forms (XXVIII.1, pp. 308–12).

8. נְקַלָּה

9. הֵחֵל

10. הֲרֵעוֹתָ
Instead of *הֲרִעוֹתָ (XXVIII.3.a, note ii, p. 315).

11. אָחֵל

12. מֵחֵל
Note that with geminate roots the initial מ of the Hiphil participle lacks the characteristic *páṯaḥ* (e.g., מַקְטִל; XVI.12, pp. 188–89).

13. אָרוֹתִי

14. הַחִלּוֹתָ

15. הֵחֵל

16. יָחֵל

17. אֹרוּ

18. יֵרַע
Again, do not overlook the Type B Qal geminate verbs (XXVIII.1, pp. 308–12).

19. יֵרוֹעַ

20. יָרֵעַ

28.b. Ruth 1.

Study tip: This text affords the student another opportunity to become reacquainted with the feminine verbal forms and pronominal suffixes.

v 1: בֵּית לֶחֶם place name—מוֹאָב place name.

v 2: אֶפְרָתִים "Ephraimites."

v 4: וַיִּשְׂאוּ Remember the frequent loss of the strong *dāgēš* to "Sqnmlwy" (VI.7, p. 59); for the meaning of this verb in its context, see BDB נָשָׂא Qal 3.d, p. 671—מֹאֲבִיּוֹת "Moabites" fem.; compare note on v 1—כְּעֶשֶׂר Quantitative use of preposition כְּ not uncommon (BDB כְּ 1.a, p. 453).

v 8: עִמָּכֶם and עֲשִׂיתֶם Masculine pronouns will sometimes function as "inclusive" pronouns.

v 9: מְצֶאןָ Defective spelling of מְצֶאנָה.

v 11: וְהָיוּ לָכֶם "that you might have."

v 12: לֵכְןָ Defective spelling of תִקְוָה—לֵכְנָה To find root, consider IV.3.b.ii, p. 34.

v 13: הֲלָהֵן The element לָהֵן is a particle not yet encountered; see BDB.

v 17: יֹסִיף ... כֹּה an important formula (XXVII.8.c, p. 305).

v 19: וַתֵּהֹם To find the root, consider XXVI.4.d, p. 293, then recall also compensatory lengthening (IV.2.a.i, p. 26).

REVIEW THE CONCEPTS

Geminate masquerade! A number of well-known biblical passages have gotten together for a masquerade ball. Each includes a difficult weak verb form that may or may not prove geminate. Translate each phrase.

1. נֵרְדָה וְנָבְלָה שָׁם שְׂפָתָם (Gen 11:7)
2. שֶׁמֶשׁ בְּגִבְעוֹן דּוֹם וְיָרֵחַ בְּעֵמֶק אַיָּלוֹן (Josh 10:12)
3. הַיָּם רָאָה וַיָּנֹס הַיַּרְדֵּן יִסֹּב לְאָחוֹר (Ps 114:3)
4. וַיָּקָם קַיִן אֶל־הֶבֶל אָחִיו וַיַּהַרְגֵהוּ (Gen 4:8)
5. עַתָּה נָרַע לְךָ מֵהֶם (Gen 19:9)
6. וַיִּדֹּם הַשֶּׁמֶשׁ וְיָרֵחַ עָמָד (Josh 10:13)
7. יִפֹּל מִצִּדְּךָ אֶלֶף וּרְבָבָה מִימִינֶךָ אֵלֶיךָ לֹא יִגָּשׁ (Ps 91:7)

8. לְכָה אָֽרָה־לִּי יַעֲקֹב (Num 23:7)
9. נְטֵה אֶת־מַטְּךָ וְהַךְ אֶת־עֲפַר הָאָרֶץ (Exod 8:12)
10 אַל־יֵרַע בְּעֵינֶיךָ עַל־הַנַּעַר וְעַל־אֲמָתֶךָ (Gen 21:12)

Answers

1. Let us go down and mix there their speech.
   Qal impf. cohortative 1cs בָּלַל; not Qal perf. fs of נָבַל.

2. O Sun in Gibeon be still, and the Moon in Ayyalon.
   Qal impv. ms דָּמַם; not דּוּם!

3. The Sea looked and fled; the Jordan turned back.
   Qal impf. 3ms סָבַב; not נָסַב.

4. And Cain arose against Abel his brother and killed him.
   Qal impf. *Wāw*-consecutive 3ms קוּם; not קָמַם.

5. Now we shall break you worse than (we would have) them.
   Hi. impf. 1cs רָעַע; not Qal perf. 3ms נָרַע.

6. And the sun was still, and the moon stood.
   Qal *Wāw*-consecutive 3ms דָּמַם; not דּוּם.

7. One thousand may fall at your side, and ten thousand at your right hand; to you, it shall not reach.
   Qal impf. 3ms נָגַשׁ; not גָּשַׁשׁ.

8. Come, curse Jacob for me
   Qal impv. ms אָרַר; not Qal perf. 3ms אָרָה. Notice that this imperative form adds the optional final ָה - (XXI.4, p. 241).

9. Stretch out your staff and strike the dust of the earth.
   Hi. impv. ms נָכָה; not Qal impv. ms הָכַךְ.

10. Let it not be displeasing to you (lit., "be evil in your eyes") on account of the lad and on account of the slave woman.
    Qal impf. juss. 3ms רָעַע "be evil, bad"; not יָרַע.

Lesson 29

In This Lesson

1. The Pual Pattern: perfect קֻטַּל; imperfect יְקֻטַּל
2. The Hophal Pattern: perfect הָקְטַל; imperfect יָקְטַל
3. The Qal Passive
4. Conditional Sentences
   real conditions introduced by: אִם, כִּי, or הֵן; rarely אֲשֶׁר
   hypothetical conditions introduced by: לֻא/לוּ or לוּלֵא/לוּלֵי

Terms to Know

apodosis
passive (VIII)
protasis
verbal pattern (VIII)

Tips

1. The Pual is the passive of the Piel. The Pual form is marked by a *u*-class vowel with the first radical and doubling of the second radical.

2. The Hophal is the passive of the Hiphil. The Hophal form is marked by a *u*-class vowel under the prefixed ה in the perfect and infinitives or with the preformative in the imperfect.

3. There are several verbal forms vocalized as Pual or Hophal that are original Qal passives. If an apparent Pual or Hophal takes the Qal as its active stem, rather than the Piel or Hiphil, that passive form is probably an original Qal Passive (see XXIX.3, pp. 323–24).

Answer Key

29.a.

1. גֹּרְשׁוּ
   The *u*-class vowel is compensatorily lengthened before ר (XXIX.1.a, note i, p. 320).

2. יְגֹרְשׁוּ

3. כֻּסּוּ

A form may take *qāmeṣ ḥāṭûp̄* instead of *qibbûṣ* as the *u*-class vowel in the first syllable (XXIX.1.a, note ii, p. 320).

4. יְכֻסֶּה
5. הָגְלָה
6. הֻכָּה (הוּכָּה in Ps 102:5)
In Hophal verbs the *u*-class vowel may be *qāmeṣ ḥāṭûp̄, qibbûṣ,* or *šûreq* with the prefix or preformative (XXIX.2, p. 322).
7. תֻּכּוּ
8. הֻכּוּ
9. הוּשַׁב
10. יוּמַת
11. מוּשָׁבִים
12. יֻלַּדְתֶּם
13. רֻאָה/רֹאָה
Due to compensatory lengthening, one would expect רֹאָה, but the only attested Pual perfect is a 3cp form vocalized as רֻאוּ in Job 33.21. This form is probably originally Qal Passive.
14. מָרְאֶה
15. יֻגַּד
16. הָחְבָּאוּ
17. חֻבְּאוּ
18. שֻׁלַּ֫חְתִּי
19. מְשֻׁלָּח
20. הָשְׁלְכָה

29.b. Jonah 1–2

Study tip: This text contains many interrogatives clauses. To review the form and use of interrogatives, see X.6, pp. 109–11.

1:3: For parsing of בָּאָה, see XIV.4.a, note iii, p. 163.

1:4: For translation of the conjunction in וַיהוָה, see XIII.4.b, p. 150—הֵטִיל. On the form, review XVI.10, p. 187.

1:7: בְּשֶׁלְּמִי = בַּאֲשֶׁר לְמִי (see dictionary under -שֶׁ, BDB -שֶׁ 4.d, p. 980; cf. vv 8, 12).

1:11: For the translation of הוֹלֵךְ וְסֹעֵר here and in v 13, see XXII.3.d, note, p. 251; see also BDB הָלַךְ 3, 4.d, pp. 232–33.

1:14: On the place and use of the נָא particle in negative commands, see XVIII.6, p. 210.

2:1: Note loss of the strong *dāgēš* after a "Sqnmlwy" letter in וַיְמַן (VI.7, p. 59; XIX.4.d. note, p. 217).

REVIEW THE CONCEPTS

Translate each sentence below and identify the condition as real or hypothetical.

1. אִם תִּהְיוּ כָמֹ֫נוּ ... וְנָתַ֫נּוּ אֶת־בְּנֹתֵ֫ינוּ לָכֶם (Gen 34:15–16)
2. לוּ הַחֲיִתֶם אוֹתָם לֹא הָרַ֫גְתִּי אֶתְכֶם (Judg 8:19)
3. אִם־יְחַיֻּ֫נוּ נִחְיֶה וְאִם־יְמִיתֻ֫נוּ וָמָ֫תְנוּ (2 Kgs 7:4)
4. לוּ יֶשׁ־חֶ֫רֶב בְּיָדִי כִּי עַתָּה הֲרַגְתִּיךְ (Num 22:29)

Answers

1. If you become like us, then we will give our daughters to you. (real condition)
2. If you had let them live, I would not kill you. (hypothetical condition)
3. If they let us live, we shall live; and if they kill us, we shall die. (real condition)
4. If there were a sword in my hand, I would kill you now! (hypothetical condition)

LESSON 30

IN THIS LESSON

1. Polel, Polal, Hithpolel
2. Pilpel, Polpal, Hithpalpel
3. Minor Patterns
4. Uses of כִּי
   causal ("because," "for")
   introduces object of perception (i.e. "I see that...")
   introduces clause stating result of an action ("so that...")
   adversative ("but")
   temporal ("when")
   conditional ("if")
   asseverative ("indeed," "surely")
   concessive ("though")
   introduces direct speech

TERMS TO KNOW

adversative
asseverative
concessive

TIPS

1. The verbal forms presented in this chapter are quite rare in biblical Hebrew. Rather than memorizing every form, it is more efficient to familiarize yourself with the basic patterns so that you can recognize them.

2. The Polel, Polal, and Hithpolel have these key characteristics (קוֹמֵם): (a) וֹ after the first radical; (b) duplication of the third radical.

3. The key characteristics of Pilpel, Polpal, and Hithpalpel are the duplication of the first and third radicals (גִּלְגֵּל).

ANSWER KEY

30.a. Isa 6

v 1: וָאֶרְאֶה This *wayyiqtōl* form appears after a nonfinite verbal construction, so its function is similar to its use after הָיָה where the הָיָה clause indicates the circumstance in which the main clause unfolds.

Here the first clause (beginning with בִּשְׁנַת־מוֹת) is temporal, denoting when the main action occurred (see *IBHS,* 33.2.4, pp. 553–54).

v 2: כְּנָפַ֫יִם Note the use of the dual form, since "wing" is associated with a paired body part (III.1.e.i, p. 19)—שֵׁשׁ כְּנָפַ֫יִם שֵׁשׁ כְּנָפַ֫יִם The repetition indicates the distributive (XXIV.7.a, p. 272).

v 9: שִׁמְעוּ שָׁמוֹעַ ... רְאוּ רָאוֹ Note the use of the infinitive absolute with the imperative (XXII.3.c, p. 250).

v 11: עַד אֲשֶׁר אִם Temporal clauses may be formed using a variety of particles. This combination identifies a later situation (*IBHS,* 38.7.a, p. 643).

Review the Concepts

The key to כִּי: Translate the following sentences and indicate the use of כִּי: adversative, asseverative (emphatic), causal, conditional, concessive, direct speech, object of perception, result, temporal. It may help to look up the passage in the Hebrew Bible to see the larger context of the phrase.

1. כִּי־תִמְצָא אִישׁ לֹא תְבָרְכֶ֫נּוּ (2 Kgs 4:29)
2. כִּי עָשִׂיתָ זֹּאת אָרוּר אַתָּה מִכָּל־הַבְּהֵמָה (Gen 3:14)
3. וְאָמַרְתָּ אֲלֵהֶם כִּי תָבֹאוּ אֶל־אֶ֫רֶץ מוֹשְׁבֹתֵיכֶם (Num 15:2)
4. הוֹשִׁיעֵ֫נִי אֱלֹהַי כִּי־הִכִּיתָ אֶת־כָּל־אֹיְבַי (Ps 3:8)
5. אַל־תַּאֲמֵן בָּם כִּי־יְדַבְּרוּ אֵלֶ֫יךָ טוֹבוֹת (Jer 12:6)
6. לֹא־עָשִׂיתִי מְאוּמָה כִּי־שָׂמוּ אֹתִי בַּבּוֹר (Gen 40:15)
7. וַיַּרְא אֱלֹהִים כִּי־טוֹב (Gen 1:12)

Answers

1. If you encounter someone, do not greet him. (concessive; may also be translated as temporal or conditional)
2. Because you did this, cursed are you among all the animals. (causal)
3. Say to them, "When you come to the land of your dwelling. . . ." (temporal)
4. Deliver me, O my God, for you strike all my enemies. (asseverative or emphatic)
5. Do not believe them, even though they speak good things to you.Z (concessive; may also be translated as conditional or temporal)
6. I did not do anything that they should have put me in the pit. (result)
7. And God saw that it was good (object of perception).

CPSIA information can be obtained
at www.ICGtesting.com
Printed in the USA
LVHW021956010719
622926LV00004B/20

9 780687 008346